FINANCIAL MARKETS SIMPLIFIED: A JOURNEY OF INSIGHTS

BY MEIR VELENSKI

Credit

Credit goes to "Driving Markets," an authoritative and dynamic platform masterfully steered by financial expert Meir Velenski. Immerse yourself in the world of daily financial market insights as Meir Velenski expertly navigates the complex terrains of global economies, providing invaluable knowledge and analysis.

With "Driving Markets," Meir Velenski takes the wheel to deliver real-time market trends, expert forecasts, and strategic investment advice. Stay ahead of the curve with precise market assessments, meticulously curated to empower investors, traders, and financial enthusiasts alike.

Unlock the power of informed decision-making as Meir Velenski effortlessly decodes intricate financial jargon into accessible language. From equities and commodities to currencies and beyond, "Driving Markets" leaves no stone unturned, guiding you on the path to financial success.

Experience the unrivaled passion and dedication of Meir Velenski, as he propels "Driving Markets" forward with unparalleled accuracy and a profound understanding of market dynamics. Don't miss the opportunity to embark on this exhilarating journey, where every turn brings you closer to lucrative opportunities and prosperous outcomes.

Drive your financial aspirations to new heights with "Driving Markets," and let Meir Velenski be your trusted co-pilot in the exhilarating world of finance.

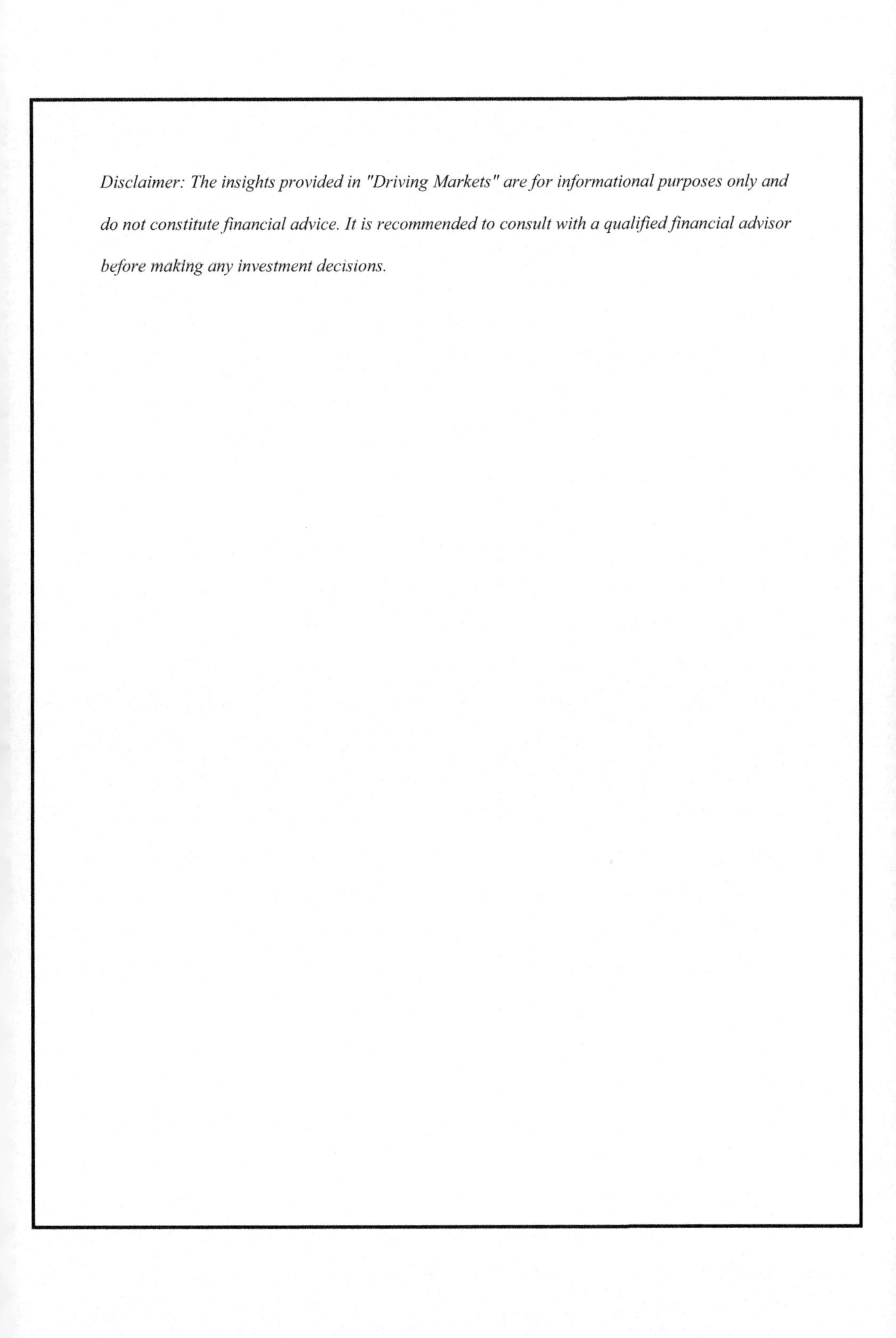

Disclaimer: The insights provided in "Driving Markets" are for informational purposes only and do not constitute financial advice. It is recommended to consult with a qualified financial advisor before making any investment decisions.

Table of Content

1: BACKGROUND INFORMATION ON FINANCIAL MARKETS

Foreword

When we think of the term "market," our minds often jump to the bustling floors of stock exchanges like the New York Stock Exchange or the frantic activity in the futures pits of Chicago. However, it's essential to recognize that these formal exchanges are just one facet of the vast financial markets, and they are not necessarily the most significant aspect.

Financial markets have existed long before the establishment of organized trading or exchanges. In fact, they have been an integral part of human civilization since the time when people settled down to cultivate crops and engage in trade. In those early days, farmers faced challenges such as poor harvests, which required them to secure seeds for the next planting season or acquire food to sustain their families. Both of these transactions necessitated obtaining credit from others who had surplus seeds or food.

Similarly, after experiencing a bountiful harvest, farmers had to make decisions regarding whether to immediately trade their surplus or store it for future use. This dilemma mirrors the choices faced by modern commodities traders in the 20th century. The exchange rates for goods during that time were highly volatile, influenced by factors like daily fish catches, crop yields, and weather conditions. The value of a basket of cassava in terms of the amount of fish it could fetch would fluctuate from day to day.

Therefore, it's crucial to understand that financial markets encompass a broader scope than just formal exchanges. They have evolved alongside human civilization, originating from the basic need for individuals to engage in economic activities such as trading, credit, and managing surpluses. The fluctuations in exchange rates and the dynamics of supply and demand have been fundamental elements of these markets since their earliest existence. The individual choices made by those farmers collectively formed a foundational financial market, serving many of the same functions as modern financial markets do today.

1.1: What is a financial market?

Generally, the financial market refers to a broad term encompassing various platforms and institutions where individuals, companies, and governments trade financial assets. It is a marketplace where buyers and sellers interact to buy, sell, and exchange financial instruments such as stocks, bonds, currencies, commodities, derivatives, and more. The financial market plays a crucial role in allocating capital, facilitating investment, managing risk, and determining asset prices.

However, the financial market has various definitions which has been evolving over time as shown below;

1. Traditional Definition: Financial markets are physical or virtual platforms where buyers and sellers come together to trade various financial assets. These assets can include stocks, bonds, currencies, commodities, and derivatives. Financial markets provide a structured environment for the exchange of capital and the determination of prices for these assets. They typically involve intermediaries such as stock exchanges, brokers, and other financial institutions that facilitate transactions and ensure market efficiency.

2. Economic Definition: From an economic perspective, financial markets serve as the conduit through which funds flow from savers to borrowers. They play a crucial role in the allocation of financial resources within an economy. Financial markets connect those who have surplus funds, such as individuals, businesses, and institutions, with those in need of capital for investment or other purposes. These markets enable the efficient mobilization of savings and facilitate productive investments, supporting economic growth and development.
3. Functional Definition: Financial markets encompass a range of functions that go beyond simple buying and selling activities. They serve as mechanisms for capital formation, allowing companies to raise funds for expansion, research, and development. Financial markets also provide opportunities for risk management, as individuals and businesses can hedge against potential losses through derivatives contracts. Moreover, financial markets facilitate price discovery, as the interaction of supply and demand determines asset prices. Additionally, they provide liquidity, allowing investors to quickly convert their investments into cash when needed.
4. Regulatory Definition: Financial markets operate within a regulatory framework established by government authorities and regulatory bodies. These regulations aim to ensure fair practices, transparency, and stability in the financial system. Regulatory oversight is designed to protect investors, prevent fraudulent activities, maintain market integrity, and mitigate systemic risks. Regulators establish rules and guidelines for market participants, monitor compliance, and enforce penalties for violations.
5. Global Definition: Financial markets extend beyond national boundaries, comprising international markets where cross-border transactions occur. These markets include the

global foreign exchange market, international bond markets, and decentralized platforms. Global financial markets enable capital flows across countries, facilitate international trade and investment, and provide opportunities for diversification and risk management on a global scale.

Each of these definitions highlights different aspects of financial markets, emphasizing their role as trading platforms, mechanisms for resource allocation, functional entities with various purposes, subject to regulation, and extending beyond national borders. Together, they provide a comprehensive understanding of the multifaceted nature and significance of financial markets in the global economy.

1.2: The Different Types Financial Markets

1.2.1: Stock Markets

Perhaps the most ubiquitous of financial markets are stock markets. These are venues where companies list their shares and they are bought and sold by traders and investors. Stock markets, or equities markets, are used by companies to raise capital via an initial public offering (IPO), with shares subsequently traded among various buyers and sellers in what is known as a secondary market.

Stocks may be traded on listed exchanges, such as the New York Stock Exchange (NYSE) or Nasdaq, or else over-the-counter (OTC). Most trading in stocks is done via regulated exchanges, and these play an important role in the economy as both a gauge of the overall health of the economy as well as providing capital gains and dividend income to investors, including those with retirement accounts such as IRAs and 401(k) plans.

Typical participants in a stock market include (both retail and institutional) investors and traders, as well as market makers (MMs) and specialists who maintain liquidity and provide two-sided markets. Brokers are third parties that facilitate trades between buyers and sellers but who do not take an actual position in a stock.

1.2.2: Over-the-Counter Markets

An over-the-counter (OTC) market is a decentralized market—meaning it does not have physical locations, and trading is conducted electronically—in which market participants trade securities directly between two parties without a broker. While OTC markets may handle trading in certain stocks (e.g., smaller or riskier companies that do not meet the listing criteria of exchanges), most stock trading is done via exchanges. Certain derivatives markets, however, are exclusively OTC, and so they make up an important segment of the financial markets. Broadly speaking, OTC markets and the transactions that occur on them are far less regulated, less liquid, and more opaque.

1.2.3: Bond Markets

A bond is a security in which an investor loans money for a defined period at a pre-established interest rate. You may think of a bond as an agreement between the lender and borrower that contains the details of the loan and its payments. Bonds are issued by corporations as well as by municipalities, states, and sovereign governments to finance projects and operations. The bond market sells securities such as notes and bills issued by the United States Treasury, for example. The bond market also is called the debt, credit, or fixed-income market.

1.2.4: Money Markets

Typically the money markets trade in products with highly liquid short-term maturities (of less than one year) and are characterized by a high degree of safety and a relatively low return in interest. At the wholesale level, the money markets involve large-volume trades between institutions and traders. At the retail level, they include money market mutual funds bought by individual investors and money market accounts opened by bank customers. Individuals may also invest in the money markets by buying short-term certificates of deposit (CDs), municipal notes, or U.S. Treasury bills, among other examples.

1.2.5: Derivatives Markets

A derivative is a contract between two or more parties whose value is based on an agreed-upon underlying financial asset (like a security) or set of assets (like an index). Derivatives are secondary securities whose value is solely derived from the value of the primary security that they are linked to. In and of itself a derivative is worthless. Rather than trading stocks directly, a derivatives market trades in futures and options contracts, and other advanced financial products, that derive their value from underlying instruments like bonds, commodities, currencies, interest rates, market indexes, and stocks.

Futures markets are where futures contracts are listed and traded. Unlike forwards, which trade OTC, futures markets utilize standardized contract specifications, are well-regulated, and utilize clearinghouses to settle and confirm trades. Options markets, such as the Chicago Board Options Exchange (CBOE), similarly list and regulate options contracts. Both futures and options exchanges may list contracts on various asset classes, such as equities, fixed-income securities, commodities, and so on.

1.2.6: Forex Market

The forex (foreign exchange) market is the market in which participants can buy, sell, hedge, and speculate on the exchange rates between currency pairs. The forex market is the most liquid market in the world, as cash is the most liquid of assets. The currency market handles more than $7.5 trillion in daily transactions, which is more than the futures and equity markets combined.1

As with the OTC markets, the forex market is also decentralized and consists of a global network of computers and brokers from around the world. The forex market is made up of banks, commercial companies, central banks, investment management firms, hedge funds, and retail forex brokers and investors.

1.2.7: Commodities Markets

Commodities markets are venues where producers and consumers meet to exchange physical commodities such as agricultural products (e.g., corn, livestock, soybeans), energy products (oil, gas, carbon credits), precious metals (gold, silver, platinum), or "soft" commodities (such as cotton, coffee, and sugar). These are known as spot commodity markets, where physical goods are exchanged for money.

The bulk of trading in these commodities, however, takes place on derivatives markets that utilize spot commodities as the underlying assets. Forwards, futures, and options on commodities are exchanged both OTC and on listed exchanges around the world such as the Chicago Mercantile Exchange (CME) and the Intercontinental Exchange (ICE).

1.2.8: Cryptocurrency Markets

The past several years have seen the introduction and rise of cryptocurrencies such as Bitcoin and Ethereum, decentralized digital assets that are based on blockchain technology. Today, thousands of cryptocurrency tokens are available and trade globally across a patchwork of independent online crypto exchanges. These exchanges host digital wallets for traders to swap one cryptocurrency for another, or for fiat monies such as dollars or euros.

Because the majority of crypto exchanges are centralized platforms, users are susceptible to hacks or fraud. Decentralized exchanges are also available that operate without any central authority. These exchanges allow direct peer-to-peer (P2P) trading of digital currencies without the need for an actual exchange authority to facilitate the transactions. Futures and options trading are also available on major cryptocurrencies

The financial market also involves various participants such as individual investors, institutional investors (pension funds, mutual funds, hedge funds), banks, insurance companies, brokers, regulators, and central banks. These participants contribute to the liquidity, efficiency, and stability of the financial market.

Overall, the financial market serves as a vital component of the global economy, providing a platform for capital formation, investment opportunities, risk management, and the efficient allocation of resources.

1.3: Who are Financial Market Actors?

The financial market involves various actors who participate in its activities. Here are some key actors in the financial market:

1. Investors: These are individuals or institutions that provide capital by purchasing financial assets such as stocks, bonds, or mutual funds. They seek to earn returns on their investments.
2. Financial Institutions: Banks, credit unions, insurance companies, and other financial intermediaries play a significant role in the financial market. They provide various services, including lending, deposit-taking, insurance, and investment management.
3. Traders: Traders are individuals or firms that engage in buying and selling financial instruments on behalf of themselves or their clients. They operate in different segments of the market, such as stock traders, currency traders (forex), or commodity traders.
4. Stock Exchanges: These are organized platforms where buyers and sellers trade stocks and other securities. Examples include the New York Stock Exchange (NYSE) and NASDAQ.
5. Brokers: Brokers act as intermediaries between buyers and sellers in the financial market. They facilitate transactions by executing orders on behalf of their clients. They may specialize in specific markets, such as stockbrokers or foreign exchange brokers.

6. Regulators: Government agencies and regulatory bodies oversee and regulate the financial market to ensure fair practices, transparency, and stability. They establish rules and regulations to protect investors and maintain market integrity.
7. Central Banks: Central banks, such as the Federal Reserve in the United States or the European Central Bank, play a crucial role in monetary policy and maintaining the stability of the financial system. They control interest rates, manage currency supply, and act as lenders of last resort.
8. Corporate Issuers: Companies or governments that issue stocks, bonds, or other securities to raise capital are important participants in the financial market. They offer these financial instruments to investors in exchange for funding their operations or specific projects.

These actors collectively contribute to the functioning of the financial market, bringing together the demand and supply of capital and facilitating the flow of funds within the economy.

1.4: What Financial Markets Do

Financial markets encompass a wide range of forms and operate through various mechanisms. Whether they are highly structured like the London Stock Exchange or more informal like street-corner money changers in African capitals, all these markets serve fundamental purposes.

1. Price setting: Markets play a crucial role in determining the value of assets, such as an ounce of gold or a share of stock. The price of an item is ultimately determined by what someone is willing to pay for it. Through market transactions, individuals buying and

selling goods establish prices, enabling price discovery and determining the relative values of different items.

2. Asset valuation: Market prices provide the most accurate reflection of a firm's value or the value of its assets and properties. This valuation is not only important for those involved in buying and selling businesses but also for regulators. For example, an insurer may appear financially sound if it values its securities at the prices paid years ago. However, assessing its solvency requires understanding the prices these securities could be sold for in the current market if the insurer needed immediate cash to cover claims.
3. Arbitrage: In countries with underdeveloped financial markets, commodities and currencies may trade at significantly disparate prices across different locations. Financial market traders seize the opportunity for arbitrage, aiming to profit from these discrepancies. As a result, prices gradually converge toward a uniform level, fostering greater efficiency throughout the entire economy.
4. Capital procurement: Firms often require funding for various purposes such as constructing new facilities, replacing machinery, or expanding their operations. Financial markets offer avenues for raising capital through instruments like shares, bonds, and other financial instruments. Additionally, individuals also rely on financial markets to obtain capital for purchasing homes, cars, or even making credit card transactions.
5. Facilitating commercial transactions: Beyond long-term capital needs, financial markets play a vital role in enabling various commercial transactions. They serve as a lubricant that facilitates activities such as ensuring payment for international product sales or providing working capital for companies to meet payroll obligations in case of delayed customer payments.

6. Investment opportunities: The stock, bond, and money markets present opportunities for individuals and entities to earn returns on surplus funds that are not immediately required. Investing in these markets allows for the accumulation of assets that can generate future income streams.
7. Risk mitigation: Derivatives contracts like futures, options, and other instruments serve as effective tools for managing various types of risks. For instance, they can provide protection against potential losses resulting from a foreign currency depreciating against the domestic currency before an export payment is received. By attaching a price to risk, these contracts enable the market participants to trade risks, allowing both firms and individuals to retain only the risks they are willing to bear while transferring or hedging the rest.

1.5: Different styles of trading

Just as there are many assets to trade, from corn to crude to antique dressers, there are lots of ways to trade them. Here's a rundown of some types of markets where price discovery takes place.

Auction markets. In auction markets, buyers and sellers meet to exchange money for goods in a structured exchange. Listed financial exchanges, such as stock markets or commodities markets, use the auction process to match the bids and offers of buyers and sellers. The U.S. Treasury also has daily and weekly auctions to sell government notes and bonds to fixed-income buyers. Wall Street is probably the first place you think of when it comes to "auction" markets; legend has it that trading there began under a buttonwood tree in 1792.

Outside of financial markets, there are other auction markets, such as those for art, wine, livestock, foreclosed homes, or a number of other assets sold at a central location, either a physical space or online. In the 20th century, Chicago became the center of the world for agricultural futures trading in a system that allowed farmers and processing companies to offset (i.e., hedge) their price risk on future prices for crops and livestock. Nowadays, a high percentage of futures market activity is in financial products such as stock indexes, Treasury securities, and foreign exchange.

Over-the-counter (OTC) markets. Unlike structured markets, OTC markets use broker-dealer networks that exist outside of an exchange to trade securities. Dealers quote prices at which they will buy or sell securities to other dealers or customers. Deals can be negotiated by phone, email, messaging services, or through electronic bulletin boards.

Several types of securities are available OTC, including stocks, bonds, currencies, cryptocurrencies, and derivatives (whose value is based on an underlying asset).

But most trades in stocks, bonds, commodities, and crypto are matched on exchanges or other trade execution platforms—a modern but much faster version of an auction market. A few decades ago, before the advent of electronic trading, trades were matched on exchange floors through an "open outcry" process. While some exchange trading still occurs via open outcry, the vast majority of transactions are done electronically.

1.6: Why is financial market important?

The financial market plays a crucial role in the economy and serves several important functions. Here are some reasons why the financial market is important:

1. Capital Allocation: The financial market facilitates the efficient allocation of capital within the economy. It connects borrowers, such as companies or governments in need of funds, with lenders or investors who have surplus capital to invest. This process ensures that capital flows to productive uses, promoting economic growth, innovation, and job creation.
2. Investment Opportunities: The financial market provides individuals and institutions with a wide range of investment opportunities. Through the market, investors can purchase stocks, bonds, mutual funds, and other financial instruments, allowing them to diversify their portfolios and earn returns on their savings. These investment activities contribute to wealth creation and long-term financial security.
3. Risk Management: The financial market offers various tools and instruments for managing risk. For example, derivatives contracts such as futures and options allow market participants to hedge against adverse price movements, reducing their exposure to potential losses. This risk management function enhances stability and confidence in the market, facilitating trade and investment.
4. Price Discovery: The financial market serves as a platform where buyers and sellers come together to determine the prices of financial assets. The interaction of supply and demand in the market establishes fair prices that reflect the perceived value of these assets. Price discovery is essential for efficient resource allocation and ensuring that market participants have accurate information for making investment decisions.

5. Liquidity: The financial market provides liquidity, enabling investors to buy and sell financial assets quickly and at a fair price. Liquidity is vital as it ensures that investors have the ability to convert their investments into cash when needed, enhancing flexibility and reducing transaction costs. Additionally, liquidity supports the functioning of other markets and the overall stability of the financial system.
6. Economic Growth and Development: A well-functioning financial market fosters economic growth and development. It facilitates capital formation by channeling savings into productive investments, enabling businesses to expand, create jobs, and innovate. Moreover, the availability of credit and financing options through the financial market supports entrepreneurial activities and stimulates economic activity.
7. Intermediation and Financial Services: Financial institutions and intermediaries, such as banks, insurance companies, and investment firms, play a vital role in the financial market. They provide crucial financial services, including lending, investment management, insurance, and risk assessment. These services promote financial inclusion, facilitate economic transactions, and contribute to the overall stability of the market.

In summary, the financial market is important as it promotes efficient allocation of capital, offers investment opportunities, supports risk management, enables price discovery, provides liquidity, contributes to economic growth, and facilitates the provision of essential financial services. It serves as a backbone of the economy, connecting borrowers and lenders, fostering economic activity, and contributing to overall prosperity.

2: THE FOREX MARKET

2.1: Overview

The foreign exchange market (forex, FX, or currency market) is a global decentralized or over-the-counter (OTC) market for the trading of currencies. This market determines foreign exchange rates for every currency. It includes all aspects of buying, selling and exchanging currencies at current or determined prices. In terms of trading volume, it is by far the largest market in the world, followed by the credit market.

The main participants in this market are the larger international banks. Financial centers around the world function as anchors of trading between a wide range of multiple types of buyers and sellers around the clock, with the exception of weekends. Since currencies are always traded in pairs, the foreign exchange market does not set a currency's absolute value but rather determines its relative value by setting the market price of one currency if paid for with another. Ex: 1 USD is worth X CAD, or CHF, or JPY, etc.

The foreign exchange market works through financial institutions and operates on several levels. Behind the scenes, banks turn to a smaller number of financial firms known as "dealers", who are involved in large quantities of foreign exchange trading. Most foreign exchange dealers are banks, so this behind-the-scenes market is sometimes called the "interbank market" (although a few insurance companies and other kinds of financial firms are involved). Trades between foreign exchange dealers can be very large, involving hundreds of millions of dollars. Because of the sovereignty issue when involving two currencies, Forex has little (if any) supervisory entity regulating its actions.

The foreign exchange market assists international trade and investments by enabling currency conversion. For example, it permits a business in the United States to import goods from European Union member states, especially Eurozone members, and pay Euros, even though its income is in United States dollars. It also supports direct speculation and evaluation relative to the value of currencies and the carry trade speculation, based on the differential interest rate between two currencies.

In a typical foreign exchange transaction, a party purchases some quantity of one currency by paying with some quantity of another currency.

The modern foreign exchange market began forming during the 1970s. This followed three decades of government restrictions on foreign exchange transactions under the Bretton Woods system of monetary management, which set out the rules for commercial and financial relations among the world's major industrial states after World War II. Countries gradually switched to floating exchange rates from the previous exchange rate regime, which remained fixed per the Bretton Woods system.

The foreign exchange market is unique because of the following characteristics:

- its huge trading volume, representing the largest asset class in the world leading to high liquidity;
- its geographical dispersion;
- its continuous operation: 24 hours a day except for weekends, i.e., trading from 22:00 UTC on Sunday (Sydney) until 22:00 UTC Friday (New York);
- the variety of factors that affect exchange rates;

- the low margins of relative profit compared with other markets of fixed income; and
- the use of leverage to enhance profit and loss margins and with respect to account size.

As such, it has been referred to as the market closest to the ideal of perfect competition, notwithstanding currency intervention by central banks.

According to the Bank for International Settlements, the preliminary global results from the 2022 Triennial Central Bank Survey of Foreign Exchange and OTC Derivatives Markets Activity show that trading in foreign exchange markets averaged US$7.5 trillion per day in April 2022. This is up from US$6.6 trillion in April 2019. Measured by value, foreign exchange swaps were traded more than any other instrument in April 2022, at US$3.8 trillion per day, followed by spot trading at US$2.1 trillion.

The $7.5 trillion break-down is as follows:

- $2.1 trillion in spot transactions
- $1.2 trillion in outright forwards
- $3.8 trillion in foreign exchange swaps
- $124 billion currency swaps
- $304 billion in options and other products

2.2: Market Size and Liquidity

The foreign exchange market is the most liquid financial market in the world. Traders include governments and central banks, commercial banks, other institutional investors and financial institutions, currency speculators, other commercial corporations, and individuals. According to the 2019 Triennial Central Bank Survey, coordinated by the Bank for International Settlements, average daily turnover was $7.5 trillion in April 2022 (compared to $1.9 trillion in 2004). Of this $6.6 trillion, $2.1 trillion was spot transactions and $5.4 trillion was traded in outright forwards, swaps, and other derivatives.

Foreign exchange is traded in an over-the-counter market where brokers/dealers negotiate directly with one another, so there is no central exchange or clearing house. The biggest geographic trading center is the United Kingdom, primarily London. In April 2022, trading in the United Kingdom accounted for 38.1% of the total, making it by far the most important center for foreign exchange trading in the world. Owing to London's dominance in the market, a particular currency's quoted price is usually the London market price. For instance, when the International Monetary Fund calculates the value of its special drawing rights every day, they use the London market prices at noon that day. Trading in the United States accounted for 19.4%, Singapore and Hong Kong account for 9.4% and 7.1%, respectively, and Japan accounted for 4.4%.

Turnover of exchange-traded foreign exchange futures and options was growing rapidly in 2004-2013, reaching $145 billion in April 2013 (double the turnover recorded in April 2007). As of April 2022, exchange-traded currency derivatives represent 2% of OTC foreign exchange turnover. Foreign exchange futures contracts were introduced in 1972 at the Chicago Mercantile Exchange and are traded more than to most other futures contracts.

Most developed countries permit the trading of derivative products (such as futures and options on futures) on their exchanges. All these developed countries already have fully convertible capital accounts. Some governments of emerging markets do not allow foreign exchange derivative products on their exchanges because they have capital controls. The use of derivatives is growing in many emerging economies. Countries such as South Korea, South Africa, and India have established currency futures exchanges, despite having some capital controls.

Foreign exchange trading increased by 20% between April 2007 and April 2010 and has more than doubled since 2004. The increase in turnover is due to a number of factors: the growing importance of foreign exchange as an asset class, the increased trading activity of high-frequency traders, and the emergence of retail investors as an important market segment. The growth of electronic execution and the diverse selection of execution venues has lowered transaction costs, increased market liquidity, and attracted greater participation from many customer types. In particular, electronic trading via online portals has made it easier for retail traders to trade in the foreign exchange market. By 2010, retail trading was estimated to account for up to 10% of spot turnover, or $150 billion per day.

2.3: Market Participants

Unlike a stock market, the foreign exchange market is divided into levels of access. At the top is the interbank foreign exchange market, which is made up of the largest commercial banks and securities dealers. Within the interbank market, spreads, which are the difference between the bid and ask prices, are razor sharp and not known to players outside the inner circle.

The difference between the bid and ask prices widens (for example from 0 to 1 pip to 1–2 pips for currencies such as the EUR) as you go down the levels of access. This is due to volume. If a trader can guarantee large numbers of transactions for large amounts, they can demand a smaller difference between the bid and ask price, which is referred to as a better spread. The levels of access that make up the foreign exchange market are determined by the size of the "line" (the amount of money with which they are trading). The top-tier interbank market accounts for 51% of all transactions. From there, smaller banks, followed by large multi-national corporations (which need to hedge risk and pay employees in different countries), large hedge funds, and even some of the retail market makers. According to Galati and Melvin, “Pension funds, insurance companies, mutual funds, and other institutional investors have played an increasingly important role in financial markets in general, and in FX markets in particular, since the early 2000s.” (2004) In addition, he notes, “Hedge funds have grown markedly over the 2001–2004 period in terms of both number and overall size”. Central banks also participate in the foreign exchange market to align currencies to their economic needs.

2.3.1: Commercial companies

An important part of the foreign exchange market comes from the financial activities of companies seeking foreign exchange to pay for goods or services. Commercial companies often trade fairly small amounts compared to those of banks or speculators, and their trades often have a little short-term impact on market rates. Nevertheless, trade flows are an important factor in the long-term direction of a currency's exchange rate. Some multinational corporations (MNCs) can have an unpredictable impact when very large positions are covered due to exposures that are not widely known by other market participants.

2.3.2: Central banks

National central banks play an important role in the foreign exchange markets. They try to control the money supply, inflation, and/or interest rates and often have official or unofficial target rates for their currencies. They can use their often substantial foreign exchange reserves to stabilize the market. Nevertheless, the effectiveness of central bank "stabilizing speculation" is doubtful because central banks do not go bankrupt if they make large losses as other traders would. There is also no convincing evidence that they actually make a profit from trading.

2.3.3: Foreign exchange fixing

Foreign exchange fixing is the daily monetary exchange rate fixed by the national bank of each country. The idea is that central banks use the fixing time and exchange rate to evaluate the behavior of their currency. Fixing exchange rates reflect the real value of equilibrium in the market. Banks, dealers, and traders use fixing rates as a market trend indicator.

The mere expectation or rumor of a central bank foreign exchange intervention might be enough to stabilize the currency. However, aggressive intervention might be used several times each year in countries with a dirty float currency regime. Central banks do not always achieve their objectives. The combined resources of the market can easily overwhelm any central bank. Several scenarios of this nature were seen in the 1992–93 European Exchange Rate Mechanism collapse, and in more recent times in Asia.

2.3.4: Investment management firms

Investment management firms (who typically manage large accounts on behalf of customers such as pension funds and endowments) use the foreign exchange market to facilitate transactions in foreign securities. For example, an investment manager bearing an international equity portfolio needs to purchase and sell several pairs of foreign currencies to pay for foreign securities purchases.

Some investment management firms also have more speculative specialist currency overlay operations, which manage clients' currency exposures with the aim of generating profits as well as limiting risk. While the number of this type of specialist firms is quite small, many have a large value of assets under management and can, therefore, generate large trades.

2.3.5: Retail foreign exchange traders

Individual retail speculative traders constitute a growing segment of this market. Currently, they participate indirectly through brokers or banks. Retail brokers, while largely controlled and regulated in the US by the Commodity Futures Trading Commission and National Futures Association, have previously been subjected to periodic foreign exchange fraud. To deal with the issue, in 2010 the NFA required its members that deal in the Forex markets to register as such (i.e., Forex CTA instead of a CTA). Those NFA members that would traditionally be subject to minimum net capital requirements, FCMs and IBs, are subject to greater minimum net capital requirements if they deal in Forex. A number of the foreign exchange brokers operate from the UK under Financial Services Authority regulations where foreign exchange trading using margin is part of the wider over-the-counter derivatives trading industry that includes contracts for difference and financial spread betting.

There are two main types of retail FX brokers offering the opportunity for speculative currency trading: *brokers* and *dealers* or *market makers*. *Brokers* serve as an agent of the customer in the broader FX market, by seeking the best price in the market for a retail order and dealing on behalf of the retail customer. They charge a commission or "mark-up" in addition to the price obtained in the market. *Dealers* or *market makers*, by contrast, typically act as principals in the transaction versus the retail customer, and quote a price they are willing to deal at.

2.3.6: Non-bank foreign exchange companies

Non-bank foreign exchange companies offer currency exchange and international payments to private individuals and companies. These are also known as "foreign exchange brokers" but are distinct in that they do not offer speculative trading but rather currency exchange with payments (i.e., there is usually a physical delivery of currency to a bank account).

It is estimated that in the UK, 14% of currency transfers/payments are made via Foreign Exchange Companies. These companies' selling point is usually that they will offer better exchange rates or cheaper payments than the customer's bank. These companies differ from Money Transfer/Remittance Companies in that they generally offer higher-value services. The volume of transactions done through Foreign Exchange Companies in India amounts to about US$2 billion per day This does not compete favorably with any well developed foreign exchange market of international repute, but with the entry of online Foreign Exchange Companies the market is steadily growing. Around 25% of currency transfers/payments in India are made via non-bank Foreign Exchange Companies. Most of these companies use the USP of better exchange rates than the banks. They are regulated by FEDAI and any transaction in foreign Exchange is governed by the Foreign Exchange Management Act, 1999 (FEMA).

2.4: Forex Pairs Explained

Currencies are always traded in pairs because when you buy or sell one currency, you automatically sell or buy another. In every currency pair, there is a base currency and a quote currency – the base currency appears first, and the quote currency is to the right of it.

The price displayed for a currency pair represents the amount of the quote currency you will need to spend in order to purchase one unit of the base currency.

For example, in the EUR/USD currency pair, EUR is the base currency and USD is the quote currency. If the quote price was 1.2000, it means that one euro is worth 1.20 US dollars.

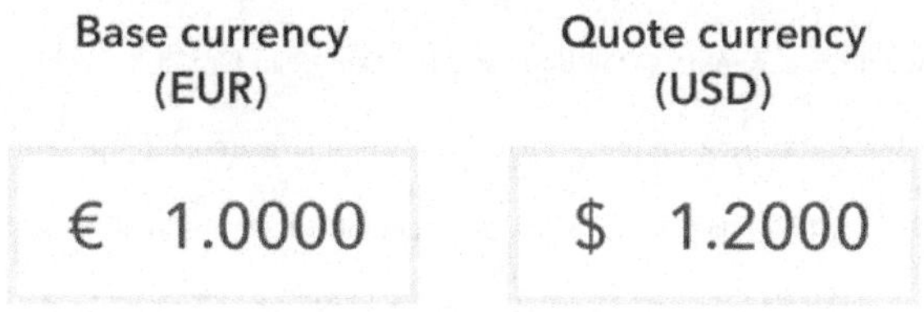

Base currency (EUR)	Quote currency (USD)
€ 1.0000	$ 1.2000

2.5: Different types of forex pairs

Broadly speaking, forex pairs can be separated into three categories. These are the majors, the commodity currencies, and the cross currencies:

- **Major currencies** are those that are most traded on the markets. Opinions differ as to how many major currency pairs there are, but most lists will include EUR/USD, USD/JPY, GBP/USD and USD/CHF
- **Commodity currencies** constitute currency pairs which have a value closely tied to a commodity such as oil, coal or iron ore. The commodity currencies included in this list are AUD/USD and USD/CAD
- **Cross currencies** are currency pairs which do not include the US dollar. Two cross currency pairs have made it into this top ten, EUR/GBP and EUR/JPY

EUR/USD

EUR/USD is the most traded currency pair on the market. The currency pair EUR/USD represents the two large economies- the USA and the European Union. It accounts for about 20% of the trading volume, resulting in tight spreads. It is among the most liquid forex pairs. The popularity of the EUR/USD pair comes from the fact that it is representative of the world's two biggest economies: the European single market and the US.

The high daily volume of EUR/USD transactions ensures that the pair has a lot of liquidity which generally results in tight spreads. Liquidity and tight spreads are enticing for traders because they mean that large trades can be made with little impact on the market.

The exchange rate of EUR/USD is determined by a number of factors, not least of which are the interest rates set by the European Central Bank (ECB) and the US Federal Reserve (Fed). This is because the currency with the higher interest rates will generally be in higher demand because higher interest rates give a better return on their initial investment. If for instance, the ECB had set higher interest rates than the Fed, it is likely that the euro would appreciate relative to the dollar.

USD/JPY

Also known as ‘the gopher’, the USD/JPY currency pair is made up of the US dollar and the Japanese yen. It is the second most traded forex pair on the market, representing 13.2% of all daily forex transactions in 2019.

Similar to EUR/USD, USD/JPY is known for its high liquidity, something it gets from the fact that the yen is the most heavily traded currency in Asia, and the US dollar is the most commonly traded currency in the world.

Much in the same way as the Fed and ECB, the Bank of Japan (BoJ) sets the interest rates for the Japanese economy which, in turn, affects the value of the yen relative to the US dollar.

GBP/USD

The currency pair GBP/USD is also known as ‘Cable’ in forex. It is due to the deep-sea steel cable between London and the New York Stock Exchange. It accounted for about 13.65% of daily forex trading volume in 2021.

Like with most other currency pairs, the strength of GBP/USD comes from the respective strength of the British and American economies. If the British economy is growing at a faster rate than that of America, it is likely the pound will strengthen against the dollar. However, if the American economy is doing better than the British economy, the reverse is true.

Historical chart of GBP/USD from 2010 to 2019

Just like the first two most popular currency pairs on this list, the quote price of GBP/USD is affected by the respective interest rates set by the Bank of England (BoE) and the Fed. The subsequent differential between the interest rates on the pound and the dollar can have a great effect on the price of the GBP/USD currency pair.

AUD/USD

The currency pair AUD/USD is also known as 'Aussie.' It takes about 7% of the daily forex trading volume. The Australian economy relies on commodities exports like iron ore and coal.

Any fluctuation in their price in the global market may influence the exchange rate. The value of the Australian dollar is tied closely to the value of its exports, with metal and mineral exports such as iron ore and coal accounting for a large proportion of the country's gross domestic product (GDP).

A slump in the value of these commodities on the world market would likely cause a reciprocal slump in the value of the Australian dollar. In the case of the AUD/USD currency pair, this means the US dollar would become stronger, so it would cost fewer US dollars to buy one Australian dollar.

Much in the same way as the previously mentioned currency pairs, the AUD/USD exchange rate is also affected by the interest rate differential between the Reserve Bank of Australia (RBA) and the US Federal Reserve. For example, if American interest rates are low, USD would probably weaken against AUD and it would cost more US dollars to buy one Australian dollar.

USD/CAD

USD/CAD is commonly called the 'loonie' on account of the loon bird which appears on Canadian dollar coins, and it represents the pairing of the US dollar and the Canadian dollar. The currency pair USD/CAD is also known as 'Loonie' for the bird on the Canadian coins. Canada earns a decent amount of dollars through their oil exports. The rise in global oil prices may appreciate the Canadian Dollar against the US Dollar. The currency pair takes up about 5% of the forex trading volume. The strength of the Canadian dollar is closely linked to the price of oil because oil is Canada's main export.

Since oil is priced in US dollars on the world markets, Canada can earn a large supply of US dollars through its oil exports. As such, if the price of oil rises, it is likely that the value of the Canadian dollar will strengthen compared to the US dollar.

USD/CNY

The currency pair USD/CNY represents the two magnificent economies of the USA and China. The currency pair takes up about 4% of forex trade. The yuan has largely been decreasing relative to the US dollar since the start of the US-China trade war. This has been due in part to the Chinese government, which has let the yuan depreciate in the knowledge that this will make the country's exports cheaper and increase their already sizable market share in countries other than the US.

USD/CHF

The USD/CHF currency pair is made up of the US dollar and the Swiss franc and is commonly known as the 'Swissie'. USD/CHF is a popular currency pair because the Swiss financial system has historically been a safe haven for investors and their capital.

As a result, traders often turn to CHF during times of increasing market volatility, but the Swiss franc will typically see less interest from traders during times of greater market stability. During times of increased volatility, it is likely the price of this pair would drop as CHF strengthens against the USD after experiencing increased investment.

Since CHF is turned to primarily during times of economic volatility or as a safe haven, it is not as actively traded as the six preceding currency pairs on this list. The currency pair USD/CHF is also known as 'Swissie.' It is popular among traders due to the stable and growing Swiss financial system.

EUR/GBP

The pairing of the euro and the British pound in the EUR/GBP pair is often seen as one of the most difficult pairs to make accurate price predictions for. This is because EUR and GBP have had a historical link given the proximity of the UK to Europe and the subsequent strong trade ties between these two economies.

The experts consider the currency pair EUR/GBP difficult to predict. Yet it takes up about 2% of the trading volume. Traders need to be cautious about interest rates and other factors after Brexit in 2020.

As with the other currency pairs on this list, traders should keep an eye on any ECB and BoE announcements which could affect the exchange rates of the euro and the pound, which would increase volatility further.

In recent years, this currency pair has fluctuated in price quite unpredictably – primarily due to the uncertainty surrounding Brexit. The high level of volatility can be attractive to traders, but it is important to have a risk management strategy in place before opening a position in a volatile market.

2.6: The Story Behind The Most Traded Currency Pairs:

Brief History of Forex

If you are a beginner in forex trading, you may wonder how this market might have started. Are you aware of the reasons behind its present-day coverage and size?

The foreign exchange began in an ancient era. Yet, for a long time, money was pegged to gold. Later, some remarkable events led to different changes.

The Bretton Woods Agreement (1944)

It was essential to reconstruct the shattered post-war global economy. Similarly, a consensus among prominent international players was necessary to promote global economic cooperation.

The Bretton Woods Agreement in 1944 established the gold standard. Also, it determined a framework for fixed international currency exchange rates. The delegates accepted the US Dollar as the backbone of international exchange.

The delegates from 44 countries agreed to establish the International Monetary Fund (IMF).

The collective regime for international currency exchange established by the Bretton Woods Agreement continued for almost three decades. Currency prices of many countries were pegged to the US Dollar, and the US Dollar price was pegged to gold during this phase.

How Free-Floating System Changed the Dynamics

In 1973, the Free-Floating System started. In this system, the demand and supply of currencies determine the exchange rates. So, a floating rate is self-correcting. The market corrects the differences in supply and demand.

After-effects of the Free-Floating System

The Free-Floating System leads to market volatility, as currency exchange rates fluctuate based on demand and supply. Strong economies with sound fiscal policies ensure stability in exchange rates. At the same time, the market sentiment towards a particular government and its policies may influence the exchange rates.

The Active Role of Central Banks Grew to Manage Currencies

But, the central banks can intervene as buyers and sellers. They balance the currency conversion rates. They buy a currency to increase demand and raise its exchange rate. They sell to push more supply to lower the exchange rate.

Central banks need not keep forex reserves to defend the exchange rate. Instead, they can use forex reserves to import capital goods. Thus, they can promote the economic growth of the respective country.

Events in the 1990s that Brought a Positive Impact

Since the 1990s, we have seen massive growth in the economy on a global scale. The adoption of technological advancements in the financial sector brought many positive changes.

Market participation became convenient. Facilitations like internet trading and the growing popularity of handheld devices were critical. Today, a person can take part in forex trading from anywhere.

The central banks, institutions, and hedge funds take up a large trading volume. The participation of individual retail traders is growing. The forex market moves a significant part of all money in the world.

2.7: Why Are Only a Few Forex Currency Pairs Popular?

Here are some factors that make major pairs in forex the most popular choice for traders:

Stability and Liquidity

Major currency pairs are from strong and stable economies. So, there would be hardly any significant fluctuations in their exchange rates. Thus, traders can trade these currency pairs with ease. There may not be any massive financial loss.

How a Country is Attractive as an Investment Destination

A government's policies to attract investments in the respective countries matter to sustain a better currency exchange rate. The aspects like ease of doing business, the attractive tax regime for new and existing investors, better infrastructure for industrialization, and excellent facilities for import and export contribute to making a nation attractive for foreign investors.

Country's Economic Growth and Net Trade Count

The overall economic growth of a country significantly affects the currency exchange rate. Major pairs represent economies possessing growing import and export, well-established business-friendly infrastructure and policies, and a considerable forex trading volume.

2.8: Why is the USD the Reserve Currency?

The US Dollar is the currency of the United States of America, the largest economy in the world. It is a powerhouse in international trade. The economic stability makes the US Dollar the most preferred currency.

The United States of America is one of the most preferred investment destinations for wide-ranging businesses. Top global companies, like Google, Meta, Amazon, and Tesla, originate from there.

As businesses flourish in this country, it has been an attractive investment destination for investors globally. The US Financial System is about 50% of the world's total finance.

It facilitates world commerce being the most redeemable currency. The US Dollar is a part of the most favoured trading pairs.

It is important to note that most central and commercial banks hold US Dollars. They keep US Dollar reserves for international transactions and investments.

That's why the US Dollar is the symbol of world currency. It is the world's primary 'reserve currency,' accounting for about 63% of currency reserves.

2.9: Interesting Facts About Forex Currency Pairs

- The total value of the global forex industry was about US$ 1.93 quadrillion in 2022. The daily turnover is about US$ 7.5 trillion.
- Kuwaiti Dinar (KWD) has the highest currency rate (Currently US$ 3.27). Though it is the world currency highest, it is not among the most traded currency pairs.
- The Iranian Rial is the world's lowest currency (Currently US$ 0.00024)
- The US Dollar is a part of more than half of forex trades.
- Experts consider EUR/USD as the best currency pair to trade. It accounts for about 20% of forex trades.

2.10: Determinats of Exchange Rates

In a fixed exchange rate regime, exchange rates are decided by the government, while a number of theories have been proposed to explain (and predict) the fluctuations in exchange rates in a floating exchange rate regime, including:

- International parity conditions: Relative purchasing power parity, interest rate parity, Domestic Fisher effect, International Fisher effect. To some extent the above theories provide logical explanation for the fluctuations in exchange rates, yet these theories falter as they are based on challengeable assumptions (e.g., free flow of goods, services, and capital) which seldom hold true in the real world.

- Balance of payments model: This model, however, focuses largely on tradable goods and services, ignoring the increasing role of global capital flows. It failed to provide any explanation for the continuous appreciation of the US dollar during the 1980s and most of the 1990s, despite the soaring US current account deficit.
- Asset market model: views currencies as an important asset class for constructing investment portfolios. Asset prices are influenced mostly by people's willingness to hold the existing quantities of assets, which in turn depends on their expectations on the future worth of these assets. The asset market model of exchange rate determination states that "the exchange rate between two currencies represents the price that just balances the relative supplies of, and demand for, assets denominated in those currencies."

None of the models developed so far succeed to explain exchange rates and volatility in the longer time frames. For shorter time frames (less than a few days), algorithms can be devised to predict prices. It is understood from the above models that many macroeconomic factors affect the exchange rates and in the end currency prices are a result of dual forces of supply and demand. The world's currency markets can be viewed as a huge melting pot: in a large and ever-changing mix of current events, supply and demand factors are constantly shifting, and the price of one currency in relation to another shifts accordingly. No other market encompasses (and distills) as much of what is going on in the world at any given time as foreign exchange.

Supply and demand for any given currency, and thus its value, are not influenced by any single element, but rather by several. These elements generally fall into three categories: economic factors, political conditions, and market psychology.

2.10.1: Economic factors

Economic factors include: (a) economic policy, disseminated by government agencies and central banks, (b) economic conditions, generally revealed through economic reports, and other economic indicators.

- Economic policy comprises government fiscal policy (budget/spending practices) and monetary policy (the means by which a government's central bank influences the supply and "cost" of money, which is reflected by the level of interest rates).
- Government budget deficits or surpluses: The market usually reacts negatively to widening government budget deficits, and positively to narrowing budget deficits. The impact is reflected in the value of a country's currency.
- Balance of trade levels and trends: The trade flow between countries illustrates the demand for goods and services, which in turn indicates demand for a country's currency to conduct trade. Surpluses and deficits in trade of goods and services reflect the competitiveness of a nation's economy. For example, trade deficits may have a negative impact on a nation's currency.
- Inflation levels and trends: Typically a currency will lose value if there is a high level of inflation in the country or if inflation levels are perceived to be rising. This is because inflation erodes purchasing power, thus demand, for that particular currency. However, a currency may sometimes strengthen when inflation rises because of expectations that the central bank will raise short-term interest rates to combat rising inflation.
- Economic growth and health: Reports such as GDP, employment levels, retail sales, capacity utilization and others, detail the levels of a country's economic growth and health. Generally, the more healthy and robust a country's economy, the better its currency will perform, and the more demand for it there will be.

- Productivity of an economy: Increasing productivity in an economy should positively influence the value of its currency. Its effects are more prominent if the increase is in the traded sector.

2.10.2: Political conditions

Internal, regional, and international political conditions and events can have a profound effect on currency markets.

All exchange rates are susceptible to political instability and anticipations about the new ruling party. Political upheaval and instability can have a negative impact on a nation's economy. For example, destabilization of coalition governments in Pakistan and Thailand can negatively affect the value of their currencies. Similarly, in a country experiencing financial difficulties, the rise of a political faction that is perceived to be fiscally responsible can have the opposite effect. Also, events in one country in a region may spur positive/negative interest in a neighboring country and, in the process, affect its currency.

2.10.3: Market psychology

Market psychology and trader perceptions influence the foreign exchange market in a variety of ways:

- Flights to quality: Unsettling international events can lead to a "flight-to-quality", a type of capital flight whereby investors move their assets to a perceived "safe haven". There will be a greater demand, thus a higher price, for currencies perceived as stronger over their relatively weaker counterparts. The US dollar, Swiss franc and gold have been traditional safe havens during times of political or economic uncertainty.

- Long-term trends: Currency markets often move in visible long-term trends. Although currencies do not have an annual growing season like physical commodities, business cycles do make themselves felt. Cycle analysis looks at longer-term price trends that may rise from economic or political trends.
- "Buy the rumor, sell the fact": This market truism can apply to many currency situations. It is the tendency for the price of a currency to reflect the impact of a particular action before it occurs and, when the anticipated event comes to pass, react in exactly the opposite direction. This may also be referred to as a market being "oversold" or "overbought". To buy the rumor or sell the fact can also be an example of the cognitive bias known as Anchoring, when investors focus too much on the relevance of outside events to currency prices.
- Economic numbers: While economic numbers can certainly reflect economic policy, some reports and numbers take on a talisman-like effect: the number itself becomes important to market psychology and may have an immediate impact on short-term market moves. "What to watch" can change over time. In recent years, for example, money supply, employment, trade balance figures and inflation numbers have all taken turns in the spotlight.
- Technical trading considerations: As in other markets, the accumulated price movements in a currency pair such as EUR/USD can form apparent patterns that traders may attempt to use. Many traders study price charts in order to identify such patterns.

2.11: Financial Instruments

2.11.1. Spot

A spot transaction is a two-day delivery transaction (except in the case of trades between the US dollar, Canadian dollar, Turkish lira, euro and Russian ruble, which settle the next business day), as opposed to the futures contracts, which are usually three months. This trade represents a "direct exchange" between two currencies, has the shortest time frame, involves cash rather than a contract, and interest is not included in the agreed-upon transaction. Spot trading is one of the most common types of forex trading. Often, a forex broker will charge a small fee to the client to roll-over the expiring transaction into a new identical transaction for a continuation of the trade. This roll-over fee is known as the "swap" fee.

2.11.2. Forward

One way to deal with the foreign exchange risk is to engage in a forward transaction. In this transaction, money does not actually change hands until some agreed upon future date. A buyer and seller agree on an exchange rate for any date in the future, and the transaction occurs on that date, regardless of what the market rates are then. The duration of the trade can be one day, a few days, months or years. Usually the date is decided by both parties. Then the forward contract is negotiated and agreed upon by both parties.

2.11.3. Non-deliverable forward (NDF)

Forex banks, ECNs, and prime brokers offer NDF contracts, which are derivatives that have no real deliver-ability. NDFs are popular for currencies with restrictions such as the Argentinian peso. In fact, a forex hedger can only hedge such risks with NDFs, as currencies such as the Argentinian peso cannot be traded on open markets like major currencies.

2.11.4. Swap

The most common type of forward transaction is the foreign exchange swap. In a swap, two parties exchange currencies for a certain length of time and agree to reverse the transaction at a later date. These are not standardized contracts and are not traded through an exchange. A deposit is often required in order to hold the position open until the transaction is completed.

2.11.5. Futures

Futures are standardized forward contracts and are usually traded on an exchange created for this purpose. The average contract length is roughly 3 months. Futures contracts are usually inclusive of any interest amounts.

Currency futures contracts are contracts specifying a standard volume of a particular currency to be exchanged on a specific settlement date. Thus the currency futures contracts are similar to forward contracts in terms of their obligation, but differ from forward contracts in the way they are traded. In addition, Futures are daily settled removing credit risk that exist in Forwards. They are commonly used by MNCs to hedge their currency positions. In addition they are traded by speculators who hope to capitalize on their expectations of exchange rate movements.

2.11.6. Option

A foreign exchange option (commonly shortened to just FX option) is a derivative where the owner has the right but not the obligation to exchange money denominated in one currency into another currency at a pre-agreed exchange rate on a specified date. The FX options market is the deepest, largest and most liquid market for options of any kind in the world.

2.12: Speculation

Controversy about currency speculators and their effect on currency devaluations and national economies recurs regularly. Economists, such as Milton Friedman, have argued that speculators ultimately are a stabilizing influence on the market, and that stabilizing speculation performs the important function of providing a market for hedgers and transferring risk from those people who don't wish to bear it, to those who do. Other economists, such as Joseph Stiglitz, consider this argument to be based more on politics and a free market philosophy than on economics.

Large hedge funds and other well capitalized "position traders" are the main professional speculators. According to some economists, individual traders could act as "noise traders" and have a more destabilizing role than larger and better informed actors.

Currency speculation is considered a highly suspect activity in many countries. While investment in traditional financial instruments like bonds or stocks often is considered to contribute positively to economic growth by providing capital, currency speculation does not; according to this view, it is simply gambling that often interferes with economic policy. For example, in 1992, currency speculation forced Sweden's central bank, the Riksbank, to raise interest rates for a few days to 500% per annum, and later to devalue the krona. Mahathir Mohamad, one of the former Prime Ministers of Malaysia, is one well-known proponent of this view. He blamed the devaluation of the Malaysian ringgit in 1997 on George Soros and other speculators.

Gregory Millman reports on an opposing view, comparing speculators to "vigilantes" who simply help "enforce" international agreements and anticipate the effects of basic economic "laws" in order to profit. In this view, countries may develop unsustainable economic bubbles or otherwise mishandle their national economies, and foreign exchange speculators made the inevitable collapse happen sooner. A relatively quick collapse might even be preferable to continued economic mishandling, followed by an eventual, larger, collapse. Mahathir Mohamad and other critics of speculation are viewed as trying to deflect the blame from themselves for having caused the unsustainable economic conditions.

2.13: Risk Aversion

Risk aversion is a kind of trading behavior exhibited by the foreign exchange market when a potentially adverse event happens that may affect market conditions. This behavior is caused when risk averse traders liquidate their positions in risky assets and shift the funds to less risky assets due to uncertainty.

In the context of the foreign exchange market, traders liquidate their positions in various currencies to take up positions in safe-haven currencies, such as the US dollar. Sometimes, the choice of a safe haven currency is more of a choice based on prevailing sentiments rather than one of economic statistics. An example would be the financial crisis of 2008. The value of equities across the world fell while the US dollar strengthened. This happened despite the strong focus of the crisis in the US.

2.14: Carry Trade

Currency carry trade refers to the act of borrowing one currency that has a low interest rate in order to purchase another with a higher interest rate. A large difference in rates can be highly profitable for the trader, especially if high leverage is used. However, with all levered investments this is a double edged sword, and large exchange rate price fluctuations can suddenly swing trades into huge losses.

3. STOCK MARKETS

3.1: What IS Stock Market?

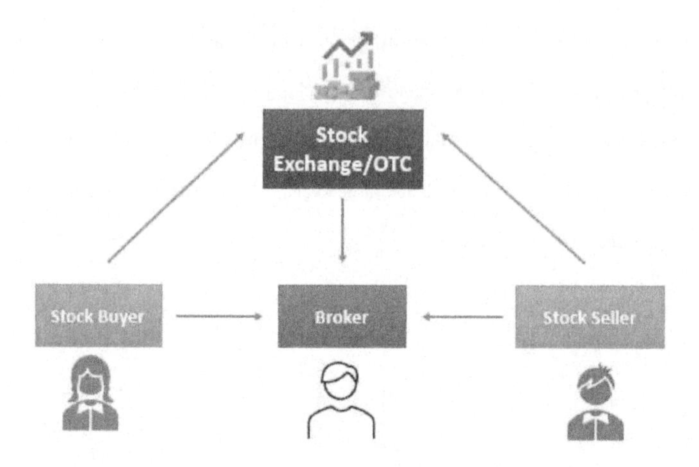

The stock market is where investors buy and sell shares of companies. It's a set of exchanges where companies issue shares and other securities for trading. It also includes over-the-counter (OTC) marketplaces where investors trade securities directly with each other (rather than through an exchange).

The stock market is a constellation of marketplaces where securities like stocks and bonds are bought and sold. Stock markets provide you with easy, transparent access to investment assets, and they help professional investors determine fair prices for public companies.

Think of the stock market as the main financial venue where investing happens. It's a collection of all the places where matches are made between buyers and sellers trading shares of public companies.

"The stock market" and "Wall Street" can refer to the entire world of securities trading—including stock exchanges where the shares of public companies are listed for sale and markets where other securities are traded. The New York Stock Exchange is the biggest stock market on earth.

Market indexes like the S&P 500 and the Dow Jones Industrial Average aggregate the prices of groups of stocks, which indicate the day-to-day performance of the stock market as a whole.

3.2: How Does the Stock Market Work?

The stock market helps companies raise money to fund operations by selling shares of stock, and it creates and sustains wealth for individual investors.

Companies raise money on the stock market by selling ownership stakes to investors. These equity stakes are known as shares of stock. By listing shares for sale on the stock exchanges that make up the stock market, companies get access to the capital they need to operate and expand their businesses without having to take on debt. In exchange for the privilege of selling stock to the public, companies are required to disclose information and give shareholders a say in how their businesses are run.

Investors benefit by exchanging their money for shares on the stock market. As companies put that money to work growing and expanding their businesses, investors reap the benefits as their shares of stock become more valuable over time, leading to capital gains. In addition, companies pay dividends to their shareholders as their profits grow.

The performances of individual stocks vary widely over time, but taken as a whole the stock market has historically rewarded investors with average annual returns of around 10%, making it one of the most reliable ways of growing your money.

3.3: Regulators of Stock Market

The Securities and Exchange Commission (SEC) regulates the stock market in the U.S. The SEC was created after the passing of the Securities Act of 1933, following the stock market crash of October 1929. SEC regulations cover four main areas:

- Stock exchanges
- Brokers and dealers
- Financial advisors
- Mutual funds

The SEC's mission is to protect investors, maintain fair, orderly and efficient markets, and facilitate capital formation. Thanks to SEC rules, companies that publicly trade on the stock market must tell the truth about their business, and those who sell and trade securities must treat investors fairly and with honesty.

3.4: Stock Market Volatility

Investing in the stock market does come with risks, but with the right investment strategies, it can be done safely with minimal risk of long-term losses. Day trading, which requires rapidly buying and selling stocks based on price swings, is extremely risky. Conversely, investing in the stock market for the long-term has proven to be an excellent way to build wealth over time.

For example, the S&P 500 has a historical average annualized total return of about 10% before adjusting for inflation. However, rarely will the market provide that return on a year-to-year basis. Some years the stock market could end down significantly, others up tremendously. These large swings are due to market volatility, or periods when stock prices rise and fall unexpectedly.

If you're actively buying and selling stocks, there's a good chance you'll get it wrong at some point, buying or selling at the wrong time, resulting in a loss. The key to investing safely is to stay invested — through the ups and the downs — in low-cost index funds that track the whole market, so that your returns might mirror the historical average.

3.5: Why Stock Market?

The point of the stock market is to provide a place where anyone can buy and sell fractional ownership in a publicly traded company. It distributes control of some of the world's largest companies among hundreds of millions of individual investors. And the buying and selling decisions of those investors determine the value of those companies.

The market lets buyers and sellers negotiate prices. This negotiation process maximizes fairness for both parties by providing both the highest possible selling price and the lowest possible buying price at a given time. Each exchange tracks the supply and demand of stocks listed there.

Supply and demand help determine the price for each security, or the levels at which stock market participants — investors and traders — are willing to buy or sell. This process is called price discovery, and it's fundamental to how the market works. Price discovery plays an important role in determining how new information affects the value of a company.

For example, imagine a publicly traded company that has a market capitalization (market value) of $1 billion, and trades at a share price of $20.

Now suppose that a larger company announces a deal to acquire the smaller company for $2 billion, pending regulatory approval. If the deal goes through, it would represent a doubling of the company's value. But investors might want to prepare for the possibility of regulators blocking the deal.

If the deal seems like a sure thing, sellers might raise their asks to $40, and buyers might raise their bids to meet those asks. But if there's a chance the deal won't be approved, buyers might only be willing to offer bids of $30. If they're very pessimistic about the deal's chances, they might keep their bids at $20.

In this way, the market can determine how a complicated piece of new information — a takeover deal which might not go through — should affect the company's market value.

3.6: Where are stocks traded?

What we call the stock market is actually many different markets around the world that trade securities like stocks and bonds. This trading typically happens on stock exchanges but can happen on other kinds of marketplaces.

1. Stock exchanges

A stock exchange is a market where an investor can trade securities in a publicly visible manner. Trading on stock exchanges is governed by rules that apply to all users of that exchange. All stock trades are now done electronically.

If a company is listed on a recognized stock exchange, it must:

- Distribute a certain number of shares.
- File appropriate information about its management team.
- Provide specific financial information.

2. Other marketplaces

Stocks are also traded through other marketplaces including:

- **Alternative trading systems (ATSs)**– automated trading systems that bring together dealers and institutional investors who trade large quantities of stocks.
- **Over-the-counter (OTC) markets** –dealer networks where "unlisted" stocks are traded.

3.7: Factors Affecting Stock Market Prices

While there are numerous factors influencing share prices, briefly explained below are some of the most crucial and decisive factors that cause stock prices to move up or down.

Demand and supply

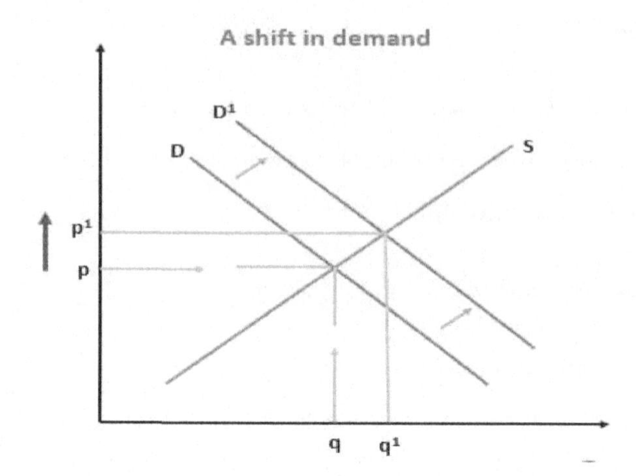

The stock market is designed to work on the age-old economic principle of demand and supply. These are the two factors that drive the price of a particular stock. When the demand for a particular stock exceeds its supply, it effectively means that the number of buyers for the stock are more than the number of sellers. This invariably leads to a rise in the price of that particular share since it signifies that the buyers are more than willing to shell out money to purchase the stock.

The converse is also true. When the supply for a particular stock is more than its demand, it essentially signifies the presence of more sellers than buyers. This drives the price of a stock downward since it indicates that the sellers are trying to get out of the particular stock, selling it at whatever price the buyers are willing to part with.

Fundamental factors

The financials of a particular company are often termed as fundamental factors. And the financial performance of a company is one of the most important factors affecting share prices. Investors will often overlook companies with weak financial performance, thereby leading to a downward spiral in the stock price. Also, traders and investors looking to generate wealth always tend to gravitate towards companies with exceptionally strong financials, which then consequently leads to an increase in demand for that particular stock, thereby driving the prices up.

Economy

Most investors tend to discount the impact of the current economic climate when predicting the price movement of shares. The state of the country's economy and the developments in the global economy are one among the many important factors influencing share prices. Stock markets are not only made up of domestic investors, but also involve a significant number of Foreign Institutional Investors (FIIs) as well.

When a country's economy shows signs of a slowdown, it discourages further investments from FIIs. Additionally, depending on the severity of the economic climate, it might also prompt FIIs into selling off their shareholdings and moving their investment into other more stable economies.

Government policies

The policies of the Government are often considered to be major factors affecting share prices in the stock market. If the policies announced by the Government are perceived as favorable by the investors, the share prices of the associated industries and sectors tend to rise. However, unfavorable policies, especially those that are concerned with taxation, can cause investors to lose faith. This subsequently prompts a sell-off, which can quickly put the share prices in a downward spiral.

Political scenario

While this might seem like an innocuous factor, in reality, it is far from it. Investors always try to stay away from investing in countries going through political uncertainty or turmoil, since such a scenario significantly increases the risk of their capital being eroded. Also, any major shift in the internal political scenario can, in the short-term, dictate the price movement of the shares in the stock market.

Dividend declarations

Although minor, declarations of dividend are meaningful factors affecting share prices in India. This is something that can be easily identified in the price chart of a particular stock. Typically, the prices of a company's stock tend to rise upon the declaration of dividend. The reason for the rise in the share price is because investors generally perceive companies declaring dividend as being financially strong and stable. However, if the declaration of dividend by a company does not meet the expectations of the investors, it increases the likelihood of the share price going down.

3.8: How to Trade Stocks as a Beginner

1. Buy the right investment

Buying the right stock is so much easier said than done. Anyone can see a stock that's performed well in the past, but anticipating the performance of a stock in the future is much more difficult. If you want to succeed by investing in individual stocks, you have to be prepared to do a lot of work to analyze a company and manage the investment.

When you start looking at statistics you've got to remember that the professionals are looking at each and every one of those companies with much more rigor than you can probably do as an individual, so it's a very difficult game for the individual to win over time.

If you're analyzing a company, you'll want to look at a company's fundamentals – earnings per share (EPS) or a price-earnings ratio (P/E ratio), for example. But you'll have to do so much more: analyze the company's management team, evaluate its competitive advantages, study its financials, including its balance sheet and income statement. Even these items are just the start.

Going out and buying stock in your favorite product or company isn't the right way to go about investing. Also, don't put too much faith in past performance because it's no guarantee of the future.

2. Avoid individual stocks if you're a beginner

Everyone has heard someone talk about a big stock win or a great stock pick. What they forget about is that often they're not talking about those particular investments that they also own that did very, very poorly over time. So sometimes people have an unrealistic expectation about the kind of returns that they can make in the stock market. And sometimes they confuse luck with skill. You can get lucky sometimes picking an individual stock. It's hard to be lucky over time and avoid those big downturns also.

Remember, to make money consistently in individual stocks, you need to know something that the forward-looking market isn't already pricing into the stock price. Keep in mind that for every seller in the market, there's a buyer for those same shares who's equally sure they will profit.

There are tons of smart people doing this for a living, and if you're a novice, the likelihood of you outperforming that is not very good.

An alternative to individual stocks is an index fund, which can be either a mutual fund or an exchange-traded fund (ETF). These funds hold dozens or even hundreds of stocks. And each share you purchase of a fund owns all the companies included in the index.

3. Create a diversified portfolio

One of the key advantages of an index fund is that you immediately have a range of stocks in the fund. For example, if you own a broadly diversified fund based on the S&P 500, you'll own stocks in hundreds of companies across many different industries. But you could also buy a narrowly diversified fund focused on one or two industries.

Diversification is important because it reduces the risk of any one stock in the portfolio hurting the overall performance very much, and that actually improves your overall returns. In contrast, if you're buying only one individual stock, you really do have all your eggs in one basket.

The easiest way to create a broad portfolio is by buying an ETF or a mutual fund. The products have diversification built into them, and you don't have to do any analysis of the companies held in the index fund.

It may not be the most exciting, but it's a great way to start. And again, it gets you out of thinking that you're gonna be so smart, that you're going to be able to pick the stocks that are going to go up, won't go down and know when to get in and out of them.

When it comes to diversification, that doesn't just mean many different stocks. It also means investments that are spread among different industries – since stock in similar sectors may move in a similar direction for the same reason.

4. Be prepared for a downturn

The hardest issue for most investors is stomaching a loss in their investments. And because the stock market can fluctuate, you will have losses occur from time to time. You'll have to steel yourself to handle these losses, or you'll be apt to buy high and sell low during a panic.

As long as you diversify your portfolio, any single stock that you own shouldn't have too much of an impact on your overall return. If it does, buying individual stocks might not be the right choice for you. Even index funds will fluctuate, so you can't get rid of all of your risk, try how you might.

Anytime the market changes we have this propensity to try to pull back or to second guess our willingness to be in.

That's why it's important to prepare yourself for downturns that could come out of nowhere, as one did in 2020. You need to ride out short-term volatility to get attractive long-term returns.

In investing, you need to know that it's possible to lose money, since stocks don't have principal guarantees. If you're looking for a guaranteed return, perhaps a high-yield CD might be better.

The concept of market volatility can be difficult for new and even experienced investors to understand.

One of the interesting things is people will see the market's volatile because the market's going down. Of course, when it's going up it's also volatile – at least from a statistical standpoint – it's moving all over the place. So it's important for people to say that the volatility that they're seeing on the upside, they'll also see on the downside.

5. Try a stock market simulator before investing real money

One way to enter the world of investing without taking risk is to use a stock simulator. Using an online trading account with virtual dollars won't put your real money at risk. You'll also be able to determine how you would react if this really were your money that you gained or lost.

That can be really helpful because it can help people overcome the belief that they're smarter than the market, that they can always pick the best stocks, always buy and sell in the market at the right time.

Asking yourself why you're investing can help determine if investing in stocks is for you.

If their thought is that they're going to somehow outperform the market, pick all the best stocks, maybe it's a good idea to try some type of simulator or watch some stocks and see if you could actually do it. Then if you're more serious about investing over time, then I think you're much better off – almost all of us, including myself – to have a diversified portfolio such as provided by mutual funds or exchange traded funds.

6. Stay committed to your long-term portfolio

Investing should be a long-term activity. You should divorce yourself from the daily news cycle.

By skipping the daily financial news, you'll be able to develop patience, which you'll need if you want to stay in the investing game for the long term. It's also useful to look at your portfolio infrequently, so that you don't become too unnerved or too elated. These are great tips for beginners who have yet to manage their emotions when investing.

Some of the news cycle, at times it becomes 100 percent negative and it can become overwhelming for people.

One strategy for beginners is to set up a calendar and predetermine when you'll be evaluating your portfolio. Sticking to this guideline will prevent you from selling out of a stock during some volatility – or not getting the full benefit of a well-performing investment.

7. Start now

Choosing the perfect opportunity to jump in and invest in the stock market typically doesn't work well. Nobody knows with 100 percent certainty the best time to get in. And investing is meant to be a long-term activity. There is no perfect time to start.

One of the core points with investing is not just to think about it, but to get started. And start now. Because if you invest now, and often over time, that compounding is the thing that can really drive your results. If you want to invest, it's very important to actually get started and have an ongoing savings program, so that we can reach our goals over time.

8. Avoid short-term trading

Understanding whether you're investing for the long-term future or the short term can also help determine your strategy – and whether you should be investing at all. Sometimes short-term investors can have unrealistic expectations about growing their money. And research shows that most short-term investors, such as day traders, lose money. You're competing against high-powered investors and well-programmed computers that may better understand the market.

New investors need to be aware that buying and selling stocks frequently can get expensive. It can create taxes and other fees, even if a broker's headline trading commission is zero.

If you're investing for the short term, you risk not having your money when you need it.

Depending on your financial goals, a savings account, money market account or a short-term CD may be better options for short-term money. Experts often advise investors that they should invest in the stock market only if they can keep the money invested for at least three to five years. Money that you need for a specific purpose in the next couple years should probably be invested in low-risk investments, such as a high-yield savings account or a high-yield CD.

9. Keep investing over time

It can be easy to dump your money into the market and think you're done. But those who build real wealth do so over time, by adding money to their investments. That means having a strong saving discipline – holding back some of your paycheck – so that you can put it to work in the stock market. You'll be able to put more money to work and grow your wealth even faster.

3.9: Risks and benefits of investing in stocks

The stock market allows individual investors to own stakes in some of the world's best companies, and that can be tremendously lucrative. In aggregate, stocks are a good long-term investment as long as they're purchased at reasonable prices. For example, over time the S&P 500 has generated about a 10 percent annual return, including a nice cash dividend, too.

Investing in stocks also offers another nice tax advantage for long-term investors. As long as you don't sell your stock, you won't owe any tax on the gains. Only money that you receive, such as dividends, will be taxable. So you can hold your stock forever and never have to pay taxes on your gains.

However, if you do realize a gain by selling the stock, you'll owe capital gains taxes on it. How long you hold the stock will determine how it's taxed. If you buy and sell the asset within a year, it will fall under short-term capital gains and will be taxed at your regular income tax rate. If you sell after you've held the asset a year, then you'll pay the long-term capital gains rate, which is usually lower. If you record a loss, you can write that off your taxes or against your gains.

While the market as a whole has performed well, many stocks in the market don't perform well and may even go bankrupt. These stocks are eventually worth zero, and they're a total loss. On the other hand, some stocks such as Amazon and Apple have continued to soar for years, earning investors hundreds of times their initial investment.

So investors have two big ways to win in the stock market:

- Buy a stock fund based on an index, such as the S&P 500, and hold it to capture the index's long-term return. However, its return can vary markedly, from down 30 percent in one year to up 30 percent in another. By buying an index fund, you'll get the weighted average performance of the stocks in the index.
- Buy individual stocks and try to find the stocks that will outperform the average. However, this approach takes a tremendous amount of skill and knowledge, and it's more risky than simply buying an index fund. However, if you can find an Apple or Amazon on the way up, your returns are likely going to be much higher than in an index fund.

4. COMMODITIES

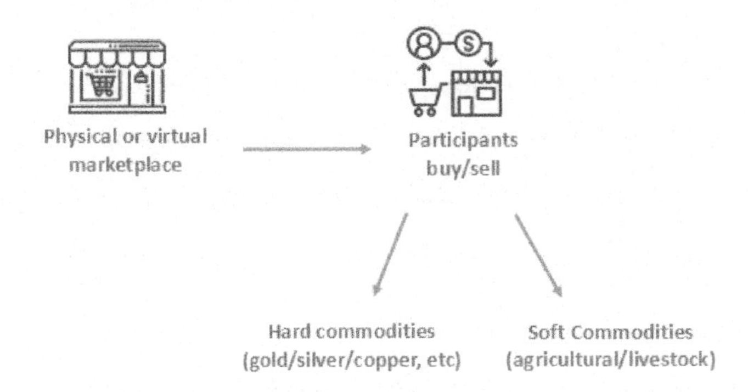

What Is a Commodity?

A commodity is a basic good used in commerce that is interchangeable with other goods of the same type. Commodities are most often used as inputs in the production of other goods or services. A commodity thus usually refers to a raw material used to manufacture finished goods. A product, on the other hand, is the finished good sold to consumers.

The quality of a given commodity may differ slightly, but it is essentially uniform across producers. When they are traded on an exchange, commodities must also meet specified minimum standards, also known as a basis grade.

Understanding Commodities

The commodity market is much older than the financial money market and has evolved. The first trading known to humanity was barter trading, where commodities like food grains would be traded between farmers and consumers. The earliest known full functional commodity market was set up in Amsterdam in early 16th

The pricing of commodities traded in the commodity market is quite complex and depends on individual characteristics. For example, the **commodity market prices** for goods like wheat and barley, a storage cost is involved in addition to the forces of demand and supply. The storage cost is required as these commodities require proper storage mechanisms to save them during transportation or from natural calamities.

There are certain criteria that a commodity must possess to be fit for trading in commodity exchanges. These characteristics are homogeneity, price fluctuations, open supply, and durability.

The **commodity market stocks** differs from money markets in terms of the underlying instrument; the underlying concepts of trading are pretty much the same. The concept of spot price, future price, expiry, and strike price are pretty much the same.

The commodity market, though, in general, trade-in generic commodities like coffee or wheat, but with time it has evolved to include certain differentiated products too. These differentiated products are generic commodities but with certain peculiar characteristics. Example of high octane gasoline for which a generic commodity would be gasoline.

Commodities are highly volatile assets compared to financial assets. They are governed not only by geopolitical tensions, economic expansions, and recessions but also by natural forces like floods or calamities.

The primary commodity exchanges in the **world commodity market** are the **London Metal Exchange**, **Dubai mercantile exchange**, **Chicago Board of Trade**, Multi Commodity exchange, etc.

Commodities are the raw inputs used in the production of goods. They may also be basic staples such as certain agricultural products. The important feature of a commodity is that there is very little, if any, differentiation in that good whether it is coming from one producer and the same commodity from another. A barrel of oil is basically the same product, regardless of the producer. The same goes with a bushel of wheat or a ton of ore. By contrast, the quality and features of a given consumer product will often be quite different depending on the producer (e.g., Coke vs. Pepsi).

Some traditional examples of commodities include grains, gold, beef, oil, and natural gas. More recently, the definition has expanded to include financial products, such as foreign currencies and indexes. Technological advances have also led to new types of commodities being exchanged in the marketplace. For example, cell phone minutes and bandwidth.

Commodities can be bought and sold on specialized exchanges as financial assets. There are also well-developed derivatives markets whereby you can buy contracts on such commodities (e.g., forwards, futures, and options). Some experts believe that investors should hold at least some portion of a well-diversified portfolio in commodities since they are not highly-correlated with other financial assets and may serve as an inflation hedge

Buyers and Producers of Commodities

The sale and purchase of commodities are usually carried out through futures contracts on exchanges that standardize the quantity and minimum quality of the commodity being traded. For example, the Chicago Board of Trade (CBOT) stipulates that one wheat contract is for 5,000 bushels and states what grades of wheat can be used to satisfy the contract.

Two types of traders trade commodity futures. The first are buyers and producers of commodities that use commodity futures contracts for the hedging purposes for which they were originally intended. These traders make or take delivery of the actual commodity when the futures contract expires.

For example, the wheat farmer who plants a crop can hedge against the risk of losing money if the price of wheat falls before the crop is harvested. The farmer can sell wheat futures contracts when the crop is planted and guarantee a predetermined price for the wheat at the time it is harvested.

Commodities Speculators

The second type of commodities trader is the speculator. These are traders who trade in the commodities markets for the sole purpose of profiting from the volatile price movements. These traders never intend to make or take delivery of the actual commodity when the futures contract expires.

Many of the futures markets are very liquid and have a high degree of daily range and volatility, making them very tempting markets for intraday traders. Many of the index futures are used by brokerages and portfolio managers to offset risk. Also, since commodities do not typically trade in tandem with equity and bond markets, some commodities can be used effectively to diversify an investment portfolio.

Special Considerations

Commodity prices typically rise when inflation accelerates, which is why investors often flock to them for their protection during times of increased inflation—particularly unexpected inflation. As the demand for goods and services increases, the price of goods and services rises, and commodities are what's used to produce those goods and services.

Because commodities prices often rise with inflation, this asset class can often serve as a hedge against the decreased buying power of the currency.

What Is the Relationship Between Commodities and Derivatives?

The modern commodities market relies heavily on derivative securities, such as futures contracts and forward contracts. Buyers and sellers can transact with one another easily and in large volumes without needing to exchange the physical commodities themselves. Many buyers and sellers of commodity derivatives do so to speculate on the price movements of the underlying commodities for purposes such as risk hedging and inflation protection.

What Determines Commodity Prices?

Like all assets, commodity prices are ultimately determined by supply and demand. For example, a booming economy might lead to increased demand for oil and other energy commodities. Supply and demand for commodities can be impacted in many ways, such as economic shocks, natural disasters, and investor appetite (investors may purchase commodities as an inflation hedge if they expect inflation to rise).

What Is the Difference Between a Commodity and a Security or Asset?

Commodities are physical products that are meant to be consumed or used in the production process. Assets, on the other hand, are goods that are not consumed through their use. For instance, money or a piece of machinery are used for productive purposes, but persist as they are used. A security is a financial instrument that is not a physical product. It is a legal representation (e.g., a contract or claim) that represents certain cash flows generated from various activities (such as a stock representing the future cash flows of a business).

What Are the Types of Commodities?

Hard Commodities

Hard commodities consist of the commodities that are required by the manufacturing industries. These should be mined and manually extracted from the land or the ocean. They have limited reserves and are most affected by geopolitical and economic conditions. Examples of such commodities are Gold, Oil, silver, rubber, copper, etc. The major part of the pricing is because of the process of extracting them.

Soft Commodities

Soft commodities constitute the commodities that are mainly Agri related or livestock. Unlike hard commodities, they are not mined or extracted but are produced through proper procedures. They have virtually unlimited reserves and are not affected by geopolitical conditions but by the weather or natural occurrences. Possible examples of such commodities are corn, wheat, barley, sugar, pork, coffee, tea, etc.

How To Trade?

There are a few steps that the trader should follow in order to trade in this market.

- It is necessary to gain knowledge about the market in advance, understand its price dynamics, demand and supply, factors influencing prices and trading instruments.
- The trader should be able to select the right broker of the firm which will charge reasonable fees, provide proper trading tools, customer support and has good track record.

- Next, the trader will have to open a trading account, complete the documentation and make the required fund deposit.
- It is important to develop a proper trading plan as per the risk tolerance, preferred commodities, trading goals and risk management techniques.
- Then the trader should check the market trends, past data, economic condition, commodity market prices pattern and select the correct trading instruments like futures contract, ETF, options, etc.
- Then they should place the buy or sell order. It is important to monitor the order execution of the order and also use the risk management strategies to limit losses and diversify the portfolio.
- Finally is is always important to monitor and make adjustment to the trades as per the changes in the risk profile, market dyanmics, and learn from experiences to improve in the process.

Example

If the price of a traded commodity fluctuates, the price of the corresponding future contracts changes in sync. Consider the case of crude oil, whose prices are decided ideally by demand and supply. Middle East countries, the major oil-producing nations, tried to control crude oil prices by controlling the supply. However, in a practical world, oil prices are affected by other factors, too- the major geopolitical consideration.

For example, in the 2008 economic crisis, global growth was down, so oil futures prices should have crashed big time. However, that was hardly the case, and oil futures were at a lifetime high of $ 145 per barrel. This was mainly because investors worldwide took out their money from equity and bought commodities and futures contracts. This increased money flow led to a surge in the oil and gold futures.

Advantages

1. Hedging Mechanism: The biggest advantage of investing in the commodity market is for the producers, importers, and exporters, as it provides them with a mechanism to hedge price fluctuations. For example, a farmer can protect himself from the price fluctuations in wheat by selling his futures contract with an expiry date three months later. A retailer, on the other hand, can protect itself by buying a futures contract.
2. Fewer Manipulations: Compared to the financial market, commodity market stocks deal in proper tangible products that are raw materials for the manufacturing industries. Hence the commodity markets are governed by demand and supply and are less prone to manipulations than financial markets.

Disadvantages

1. Risky: Commodities investments are risky as geopolitical factors play an important role in pricing. For example, any suspicion of a political crisis in the middle east leads to a sudden spike in crude oil prices. Because of such a systematic risk, commodity markets are prone to operational failures and must be regularly monitored to avoid unfavorable circumstances.
2. Leverage: Unlike financial markets, commodity markets thrive on low-margin requirements and high leverage. Though it helps in better potential profit, high leverage

ratios during an economic recession or unexpected volatile movements can lead to increased losses.

6. THE BOND MARKET

You might think the stock market is huge, but the bond market is even bigger. According to the Securities Industry and Financial Markets Association (SIFMA), the global bond market was worth $126.9 trillion at the end of 2021, compared to the $124.4 trillion global equity market cap. The gap between the two has likely widened in 2023 as stock prices have fallen.

Although many stock investors may ignore the bond market, fixed income markets influence both the stock market, since bonds compete for investment dollars with stocks, and the overall economy. So it's important to understand the bond market even if you have no intention of owning bonds.

If you are considering investing in bonds, there are number of different options at your disposal, including corporate bonds, municipal bonds, treasuries, mortgage bonds, and others. In this deep dive into everything about the bond market, we'll review the different kinds of bonds, how the bond market works, how it compares to the stock market, and the pros and cons of investing in the bond market.

What is the bond market?

The bond market refers to the global exchange of debt securities. Unlike the stock market, bonds aren't typically traded on an exchange like the New York Stock Exchange. Instead, bonds are usually bought and sold over the counter through broker/dealers. That's partly because bonds have a range of maturities, coupons, and credit ratings, which makes the bond market more complex than the stock market where most companies tend to just have one class of stock available to the public.

Bonds are priced primarily according to two factors: interest rates, which determine how an existing bond compares to a new bond, and the creditworthiness of the borrower. Bond prices, especially for corporate bonds, can fall if investors are concerned that the borrower may become insolvent.

Bonds can be bought and sold in two different ways -- through the primary market and in the secondary market.

Primary market

The primary market refers to new issues of bonds. This is where bonds are originated. If you are buying a bond in the primary market, you are buying it directly from the seller, which could be a company, a government, a bank, or another financial entity that may create a financial product such as a mortgage bond.

Secondary market

On the secondary markets, bonds are bought and sold between investors through a broker. In a sense, bonds on the secondary market are traded like stocks, from investor to investor rather than from the borrower or company. Although bond prices and bond yields can change over time, their coupons and maturities do not, which means bonds generally tend to be less volatile than stocks.

Types of bond markets

Corporate bonds

The corporate bond market is made up of publicly traded and privately held companies that sell debt to finance capital projects. Corporate bonds tend to offer higher yields than other types of bonds, although yields can vary widely from company to company depending on credit ratings and current business prospects. Corporate bonds are divided into investment-grade, which includes any debt rated BBB- or better, according to the Standard & Poor's rating scale. A bond with a lower rating is called a junk bond or high-yield bond. Those will pay investors a higher coupon rate, but they also come with greater default risk.

Government bonds

Government bonds are bonds issued by sovereign nations to fund government spending. U.S. Treasuries are the most common example of a government bond. They are considered the safest bonds in the world since they are backed by the U.S. government. In fact, Treasuries are considered so secure that their yields are used to determine the risk-free rate.

Municipal bonds

Municipal bonds are sold by cities and states. Often called munis, the bonds help local governments raise money for a variety of capital projects such as roads, schools, parks, and other infrastructure. Municipal bonds tends to be riskier than government bonds but safer than corporate bonds. Occasionally, a city will default on its debt, but it's a relatively rare occurrence. In 2017, Puerto Rico filed for bankruptcy on $70 billion in debt, which is the largest public debt default in U.S. history.

Interest from muni bonds is also generally untaxed by the federal government, a bonus for investors.

Mortgage-backed bonds

Mortgage-backed bonds or mortgage-backed securities include individual mortgages that have been bundled into a bond. Mortgage bonds essentially allow fixed income investors to invest in the real estate market. The financial crisis notwithstanding, mortgage bonds have historically been a safe investment. They can be an opportunity for bond investors looking for high-yield income; interest rates for 30-year fixed-rate mortgages hovered around 7% in late 2022.

Emerging-market bonds

If you're a fixed-income investor hoping for a high yield, emerging-market bonds are the best place to look. Emerging-market bonds are bonds issued by governments or corporations in developing countries. Because debt from emerging markets tends to be riskier, emerging-market bonds tend to offer higher yields than their counterparts from developed countries. With the stronger dollar, emerging markets are under increasing pressure, meaning yields are likely to rise.

Bond market vs. stock market

The stock market and bond market represent the two main ways businesses raise cash, through equity or debt. Both stocks and bonds give investors and opportunity to collect recurring payments. In stocks, these are called dividends; with bonds, they're coupons. However, with bonds, the purpose of investing is generally to collect the coupon, although investors will be paid back the principal of the bond when it reaches maturity. Some stocks pay dividends, but the price of a stock is generally much more volatile than it is with bonds, so stock investors usually get most of their return from price appreciation rather than dividends.

The bond market and stock market also influence each other. Higher interest rates tend to make bonds more attractive, pulling money out of the stock market and into bonds. The reverse is true in a low-rate environment.

Stocks in general are riskier than bonds, with more upside and downside, so they attract more risk-tolerant investors. Whether you choose to invest in stocks or bonds will likely be determined in part by your time horizon. Financial advisors often recommend a portfolio that shifts from stocks to bonds as the investor approaches retirement. Moving money from stocks to bonds also helps preserve capital, although you lose the opportunity for higher gains.

7. CRYPTOCURRENCY MARKET

Cryptocurrency – meaning and definition

Cryptocurrency, sometimes called crypto-currency or crypto, is any form of currency that exists digitally or virtually and uses cryptography to secure transactions. Cryptocurrencies don't have a central issuing or regulating authority, instead using a decentralized system to record transactions and issue new units.

What is cryptocurrency?

Cryptocurrency is a digital payment system that doesn't rely on banks to verify transactions. It's a peer-to-peer system that can enable anyone anywhere to send and receive payments. Instead of being physical money carried around and exchanged in the real world, cryptocurrency payments exist purely as digital entries to an online database describing specific transactions. When you transfer cryptocurrency funds, the transactions are recorded in a public ledger. Cryptocurrency is stored in digital wallets.

Cryptocurrency received its name because it uses encryption to verify transactions. This means advanced coding is involved in storing and transmitting cryptocurrency data between wallets and to public ledgers. The aim of encryption is to provide security and safety.

The first cryptocurrency was Bitcoin, which was founded in 2009 and remains the best known today. Much of the interest in cryptocurrencies is to trade for profit, with speculators at times driving prices skyward.

How does cryptocurrency work?

Cryptocurrencies run on a distributed public ledger called blockchain, a record of all transactions updated and held by currency holders.

Units of cryptocurrency are created through a process called mining, which involves using computer power to solve complicated mathematical problems that generate coins. Users can also buy the currencies from brokers, then store and spend them using cryptographic wallets.

If you own cryptocurrency, you don't own anything tangible. What you own is a key that allows you to move a record or a unit of measure from one person to another without a trusted third party.

Although Bitcoin has been around since 2009, cryptocurrencies and applications of blockchain technology are still emerging in financial terms, and more uses are expected in the future.

Transactions including bonds, stocks, and other financial assets could eventually be traded using the technology.

Cryptocurrency examples

There are thousands of cryptocurrencies. Some of the best known include:

Bitcoin:

Founded in 2009, Bitcoin was the first cryptocurrency and is still the most commonly traded. The currency was developed by Satoshi Nakamoto – widely believed to be a pseudonym for an individual or group of people whose precise identity remains unknown.

Ethereum:

Developed in 2015, Ethereum is a blockchain platform with its own cryptocurrency, called Ether (ETH) or Ethereum. It is the most popular cryptocurrency after Bitcoin.

Litecoin:

This currency is most similar to bitcoin but has moved more quickly to develop new innovations, including faster payments and processes to allow more transactions.

Ripple:

Ripple is a distributed ledger system that was founded in 2012. Ripple can be used to track different kinds of transactions, not just cryptocurrency. The company behind it has worked with various banks and financial institutions.

Non-Bitcoin cryptocurrencies are collectively known as "altcoins" to distinguish them from the original.

How to buy cryptocurrency

You may be wondering how to buy cryptocurrency safely. There are typically three steps involved. These are:

Step 1: Choosing a platform

The first step is deciding which platform to use. Generally, you can choose between a traditional broker or dedicated cryptocurrency exchange:

- **Traditional brokers.** These are online brokers who offer ways to buy and sell cryptocurrency, as well as other financial assets like stocks, bonds, and ETFs. These platforms tend to offer lower trading costs but fewer crypto features.
- **Cryptocurrency exchanges.** There are many cryptocurrency exchanges to choose from, each offering different cryptocurrencies, wallet storage, interest-bearing account options, and more. Many exchanges charge asset-based fees.

When comparing different platforms, consider which cryptocurrencies are on offer, what fees they charge, their security features, storage and withdrawal options, and any educational resources.

Step 2: Funding your account

Once you have chosen your platform, the next step is to fund your account so you can begin trading. Most crypto exchanges allow users to purchase crypto using fiat (i.e., government-issued) currencies such as the US Dollar, the British Pound, or the Euro using their debit or credit cards – although this varies by platform.

Crypto purchases with credit cards are considered risky, and some exchanges don't support them. Some credit card companies don't allow crypto transactions either. This is because cryptocurrencies are highly volatile, and it is not advisable to risk going into debt — or potentially paying high credit card transaction fees — for certain assets.

Some platforms will also accept ACH transfers and wire transfers. The accepted payment methods and time taken for deposits or withdrawals differ per platform. Equally, the time taken for deposits to clear varies by payment method.

An important factor to consider is fees. These include potential deposit and withdrawal transaction fees plus trading fees. Fees will vary by payment method and platform, which is something to research at the outset.

Step 3: Placing an order

You can place an order via your broker's or exchange's web or mobile platform. If you are planning to buy cryptocurrencies, you can do so by selecting "buy," choosing the order type, entering the amount of cryptocurrencies you want to purchase, and confirming the order. The same process applies to "sell" orders.

There are also other ways to invest in crypto. These include payment services like PayPal, Cash App, and Venmo, which allow users to buy, sell, or hold cryptocurrencies. In addition, there are the following investment vehicles:

- **Bitcoin trusts:** You can buy shares of Bitcoin trusts with a regular brokerage account. These vehicles give retail investors exposure to crypto through the stock market.
- **Bitcoin mutual funds:** There are Bitcoin ETFs and Bitcoin mutual funds to choose from.
- **Blockchain stocks or ETFs:** You can also indirectly invest in crypto through blockchain companies that specialize in the technology behind crypto and crypto transactions. Alternatively, you can buy stocks or ETFs of companies that use blockchain technology.

How to store cryptocurrency

Once you have purchased cryptocurrency, you need to store it safely to protect it from hacks or theft. Usually, cryptocurrency is stored in crypto wallets, which are physical devices or online software used to store the private keys to your cryptocurrencies securely. Some exchanges provide wallet services, making it easy for you to store directly through the platform. However, not all exchanges or brokers automatically provide wallet services for you.

There are different wallet providers to choose from. The terms "hot wallet" and "cold wallet" are used:

- **Hot wallet storage:** "hot wallets" refer to crypto storage that uses online software to protect the private keys to your assets.

- **Cold wallet storage:** Unlike hot wallets, cold wallets (also known as hardware wallets) rely on offline electronic devices to securely store your private keys.

What can you buy with cryptocurrency?

When it was first launched, Bitcoin was intended to be a medium for daily transactions, making it possible to buy everything from a cup of coffee to a computer or even big-ticket items like real estate. That hasn't quite materialized and, while the number of institutions accepting cryptocurrencies is growing, large transactions involving it are rare. Even so, it is possible to buy a wide variety of products from e-commerce websites using crypto. Here are some examples:

Technology and e-commerce sites:

Several companies that sell tech products accept crypto on their websites, such as newegg.com, AT&T, and Microsoft. Overstock, an e-commerce platform, was among the first sites to accept Bitcoin. Shopify, Rakuten, and Home Depot also accept it.

Luxury goods:

Some luxury retailers accept crypto as a form of payment. For example, online luxury retailer Bitdials offers Rolex, Patek Philippe, and other high-end watches in return for Bitcoin.

Cars:

Some car dealers – from mass-market brands to high-end luxury dealers – already accept cryptocurrency as payment.

Insurance:

In April 2021, Swiss insurer AXA announced that it had begun accepting Bitcoin as a mode of payment for all its lines of insurance except life insurance (due to regulatory issues). Premier Shield Insurance, which sells home and auto insurance policies in the US, also accepts Bitcoin for premium payments.

If you want to spend cryptocurrency at a retailer that doesn't accept it directly, you can use a cryptocurrency debit card, such as BitPay in the US.

Cryptocurrency fraud and cryptocurrency scams

Unfortunately, cryptocurrency crime is on the rise. Cryptocurrency scams include:

Fake websites: Bogus sites which feature fake testimonials and crypto jargon promising massive, guaranteed returns, provided you keep investing.

Virtual Ponzi schemes: Cryptocurrency criminals promote non-existent opportunities to invest in digital currencies and create the illusion of huge returns by paying off old investors with new investors' money. One scam operation, BitClub Network, raised more than $700 million before its perpetrators were indicted in December 2019.

"Celebrity" endorsements: Scammers pose online as billionaires or well-known names who promise to multiply your investment in a virtual currency but instead steal what you send. They may also use messaging apps or chat rooms to start rumours that a famous businessperson is backing a specific cryptocurrency. Once they have encouraged investors to buy and driven up the price, the scammers sell their stake, and the currency reduces in value.

Romance scams: The FBI warns of a trend in online dating scams, where tricksters persuade people they meet on dating apps or social media to invest or trade in virtual currencies. The FBI's Internet Crime Complaint Centre fielded more than 1,800 reports of crypto-focused romance scams in the first seven months of 2021, with losses reaching $133 million.

Otherwise, fraudsters may pose as legitimate virtual currency traders or set up bogus exchanges to trick people into giving them money. Another crypto scam involves fraudulent sales pitches for individual retirement accounts in cryptocurrencies. Then there is straightforward cryptocurrency hacking, where criminals break into the digital wallets where people store their virtual currency to steal it.

Is cryptocurrency safe?

Cryptocurrencies are usually built using blockchain technology. Blockchain describes the way transactions are recorded into "blocks" and time stamped. It's a fairly complex, technical process, but the result is a digital ledger of cryptocurrency transactions that's hard for hackers to tamper with.

In addition, transactions require a two-factor authentication process. For instance, you might be asked to enter a username and password to start a transaction. Then, you might have to enter an authentication code sent via text to your personal cell phone.

While securities are in place, that does not mean cryptocurrencies are un-hackable. Several high-dollar hacks have cost cryptocurrency start-ups heavily. Hackers hit Coincheck to the tune of $534 million and BitGrail for $195 million, making them two of the biggest cryptocurrency hacks of 2018.

Unlike government-backed money, the value of virtual currencies is driven entirely by supply and demand. This can create wild swings that produce significant gains for investors or big losses. And cryptocurrency investments are subject to far less regulatory protection than traditional financial products like stocks, bonds, and mutual funds.

Four tips to invest in cryptocurrency safely

According to Consumer Reports, all investments carry risk, but some experts consider cryptocurrency to be one of the riskier investment choices out there. If you are planning to invest in cryptocurrencies, these tips can help you make educated choices.

Research exchanges:

Before you invest, learn about cryptocurrency exchanges. It's estimated that there are over 500 exchanges to choose from. Do your research, read reviews, and talk with more experienced investors before moving forward.

Know how to store your digital currency:

If you buy cryptocurrency, you have to store it. You can keep it on an exchange or in a digital wallet. While there are different kinds of wallets, each has its benefits, technical requirements, and security. As with exchanges, you should investigate your storage choices before investing.

Diversify your investments:

Diversification is key to any good investment strategy, and this holds true when you are investing in cryptocurrency. Don't put all your money in Bitcoin, for example, just because that's the name you know. There are thousands of options, and it's better to spread your investment across several currencies.

Prepare for volatility:

The cryptocurrency market is highly volatile, so be prepared for ups and downs. You will see dramatic swings in prices. If your investment portfolio or mental wellbeing can't handle that, cryptocurrency might not be a wise choice for you.

Cryptocurrency is all the rage right now, but remember, it is still in its relative infancy and is considered highly speculative. Investing in something new comes with challenges, so be prepared. If you plan to participate, do your research, and invest conservatively to start.

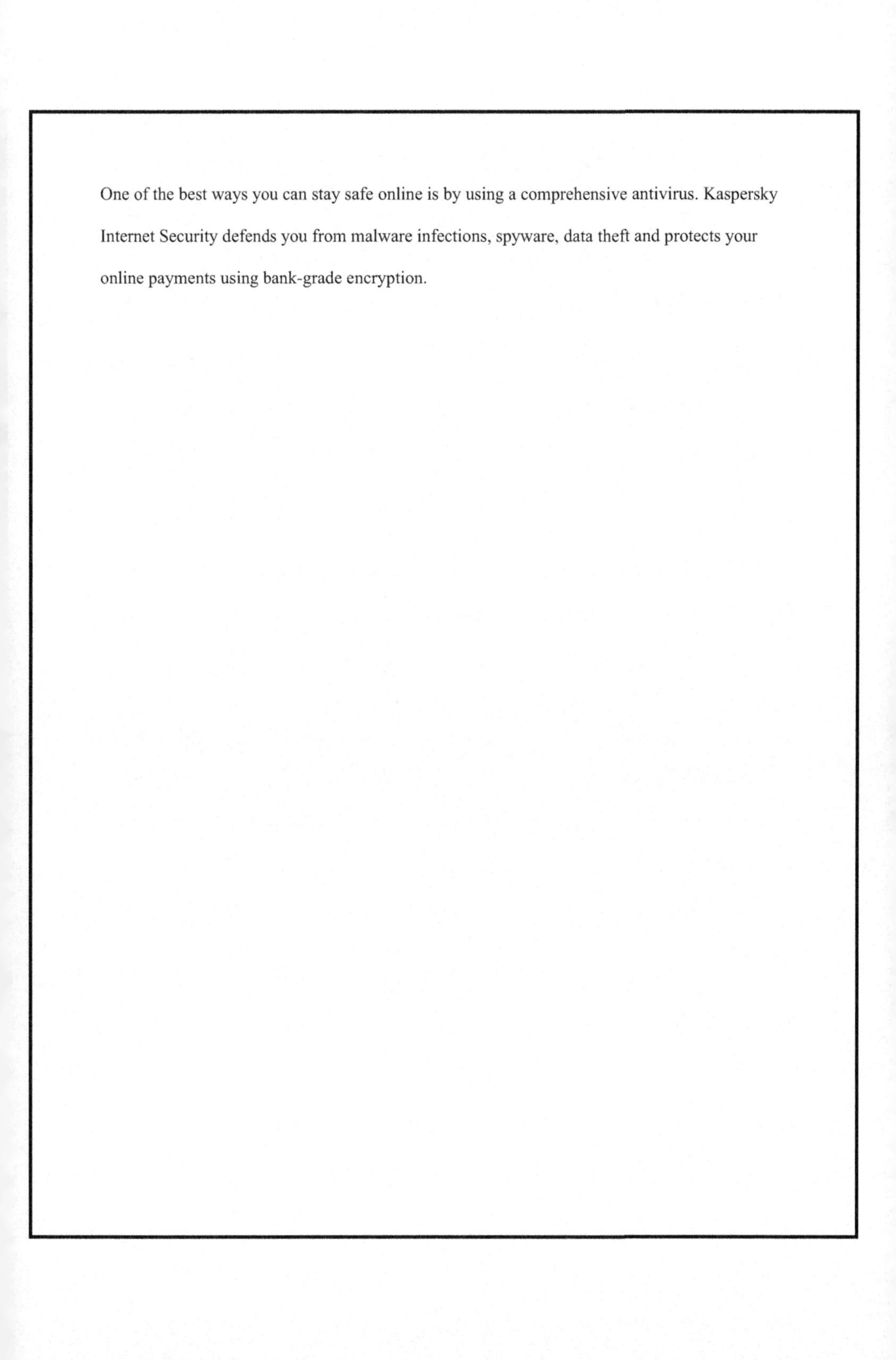

One of the best ways you can stay safe online is by using a comprehensive antivirus. Kaspersky Internet Security defends you from malware infections, spyware, data theft and protects your online payments using bank-grade encryption.

8. ROLE OF BANKS IN THE FINANCIAL MARKETS

Banks play a central and vital role in the financial markets. Their functions and activities are diverse, and they serve as key intermediaries between various participants in the economy. Some of the essential roles of banks in the financial markets include:

1. Mobilizing and Intermediating Funds: Banks accept deposits from individuals, businesses, and institutions and use these funds to provide loans and credit to borrowers. By channeling savings into investments, banks facilitate capital formation and support economic growth.
2. Providing Credit and Capital: Banks are major lenders in the financial markets, offering various types of credit facilities, including personal loans, mortgages, business loans, and working capital to businesses. They also help companies raise capital through underwriting and facilitating the issuance of bonds and stocks.
3. Facilitating Payments and Settlements: Banks act as facilitators of financial transactions, offering services such as electronic fund transfers, check clearing, and online payment systems. They play a critical role in ensuring smooth and efficient payment and settlement processes between different parties.
4. Risk Management and Hedging: Banks provide financial products and services that help clients manage and mitigate risks. This includes offering insurance products, derivatives, and hedging strategies to protect against adverse price movements and market fluctuations.

5. Market Making and Trading: Many banks engage in market-making activities, especially in the foreign exchange and securities markets. They buy and sell financial instruments to provide liquidity and ensure smooth trading in these markets.
6. Wealth Management and Investment Services: Banks offer wealth management services, providing advice and investment solutions to individuals and institutional clients to grow and preserve their assets.
7. Investment Banking: Banks play a significant role in investment banking activities, such as mergers and acquisitions, initial public offerings (IPOs), and corporate restructuring. They act as intermediaries between companies seeking capital and investors looking for investment opportunities.
8. Research and Analysis: Banks provide valuable research and market analysis to investors and clients. Their research reports and insights help inform investment decisions and shape market trends.
9. Regulated Financial Intermediaries: Banks are subject to strict regulatory oversight, ensuring their stability, solvency, and compliance with financial laws and regulations. This helps maintain confidence in the financial system and protects the interests of depositors and investors.

Overall, banks are critical players in the financial markets, connecting savers and borrowers, facilitating economic activity, and contributing to the efficient functioning of the broader economy. Their roles extend across various sectors, making them an integral part of the financial ecosystem.

For instance, Goldman Sachs, JP Morgan, Barclays, and Deutsche Bank are major global financial institutions that play significant roles in the financial markets. Each of these banks has a broad and diverse range of operations and services, making them key players in various aspects of the financial industry. Here is an overview of their involvement in the financial markets:

1. Goldman Sachs:
    - Investment Banking: Goldman Sachs is renowned for its investment banking division, providing advisory services for mergers and acquisitions, underwriting securities offerings, and assisting companies in raising capital through IPOs.
    - Trading and Sales: The bank is heavily involved in trading activities, including equities, fixed income, currencies, and commodities, catering to institutional clients and investors.
    - Asset Management: Goldman Sachs operates an asset management division, offering investment management services to institutional and individual clients, including mutual funds, hedge funds, and private equity.
2. JP Morgan:
    - Corporate and Investment Banking: JP Morgan is a leading provider of corporate and investment banking services, offering mergers and acquisitions advisory, debt and equity financing, and treasury services to corporations and institutions worldwide.
    - Asset Management: The bank's asset management division manages investment portfolios for clients, including pension funds, endowments, and individual investors, with a broad range of investment products.

- Commercial Banking: JP Morgan provides banking services to businesses, governments, and institutions, offering cash management, trade finance, and treasury services.

3. Barclays:
   - Retail and Commercial Banking: Barclays operates retail and commercial banking services, serving individuals and businesses with checking and savings accounts, loans, and other financial products.
   - Investment Banking: Barclays is involved in investment banking activities, providing corporate finance advisory, capital raising, and trading services.
   - Wealth Management: The bank offers wealth management services, catering to high-net-worth individuals with investment management and financial planning solutions.
4. Deutsche Bank:
   - Corporate Banking: Deutsche Bank provides a wide range of corporate banking services, including trade finance, cash management, and foreign exchange solutions for businesses and institutions.
   - Investment Banking: The bank has a strong presence in investment banking, offering advisory services, debt and equity capital raising, and securities trading.
   - Asset Management: Deutsche Bank's asset management division manages investment portfolios and offers mutual funds and other investment products to clients.

These financial institutions are among the largest and most influential in the world, and their involvement in the financial markets spans a broad spectrum of services. They contribute significantly to the global financial landscape, playing key roles in capital allocation, risk management, and supporting economic growth.

9. CHOOSING THE RIGHT MARKET

Choosing which markets to trade can be a crucial decision that significantly impacts your trading success. Consider the following factors to help guide your decision-making process:

1. Market Knowledge and Expertise: Focus on markets that align with your knowledge, expertise, and interests. Trading in markets you understand well can give you a competitive advantage and improve your ability to analyze and predict price movements.
2. Risk Tolerance: Assess your risk tolerance and trading style. Some markets may be more volatile and carry higher risks than others. Determine how much risk you are comfortable with and choose markets that match your risk appetite.
3. Market Liquidity: Opt for liquid markets with substantial trading volumes. Higher liquidity ensures that you can easily enter and exit positions without significant slippage or price fluctuations.
4. Accessibility and Trading Hours: Consider the accessibility of the market and its trading hours. Some markets may have limited trading hours or may not be accessible due to geographical restrictions.
5. Trading Costs: Evaluate the trading costs associated with each market, including spreads, commissions, and other fees. Lower trading costs can enhance your profitability over time.

6. Diversification: Diversifying your portfolio across different markets can help spread risk and reduce the impact of potential losses in one market.
7. Economic and Geopolitical Factors: Keep an eye on economic indicators, geopolitical events, and market news that can influence specific markets. Understanding how these factors affect your chosen markets can help you make informed trading decisions.
8. Trading Tools and Platforms: Ensure that you have access to reliable trading tools and platforms that support your chosen markets and trading strategies.
9. Market Trends and Volatility: Analyze market trends and historical volatility. Consider how your trading strategy aligns with the market conditions of your chosen assets.
10. Long-term vs. Short-term Trading: Decide whether you prefer long-term or short-term trading. Some markets may be better suited for day trading, while others are more appropriate for longer-term positions.
11. Regulatory Environment: Familiarize yourself with the regulatory environment of the markets you intend to trade in. Different markets may have varying levels of oversight and regulations that could impact your trading activities.

Remember that trading involves risks, and no market is entirely predictable. It's essential to continuously educate yourself, practice risk management, and adapt your approach based on market conditions and your trading experiences. Always start with a small capital allocation and gradually scale up as you gain confidence and proficiency in your chosen markets.

TRENDS IN THE FINANCIAL MARKETS

2023 will be a challenging year for financial institutions. Innovative new technologies are redefining the sector, shaping the services that financial organisations offer, the ways in which they interact with consumers, and the ways in which they apply new sources of data across departments. But the onset of growing economic instability is putting entire markets in jeopardy and threatening to yield mounting uncertainty for lenders and borrowers alike.

Nevertheless, the evolution of financial services is set to continue. Let's examine the 4 top trends for financial organisations in 2023:

1. Open banking will dominate the future
2. Cloud-native systems will replace legacy alternatives
3. Artificial intelligence (AI) and machine learning (ML) will increase in importance
4. Cybersecurity continues as a top priority

1. Open Banking will dominate the future

According to Statista, the number of global open banking users "is expected to grow at an average annual rate of nearly 50 percent between 2020 and 2024, with the European market being the largest". Considering how open data benefits consumers as well as financial players, it's easy to understand why this trend will become increasingly popular moving forward.

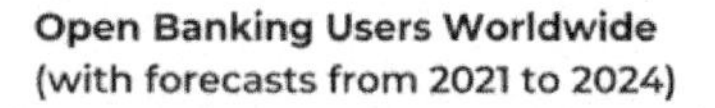

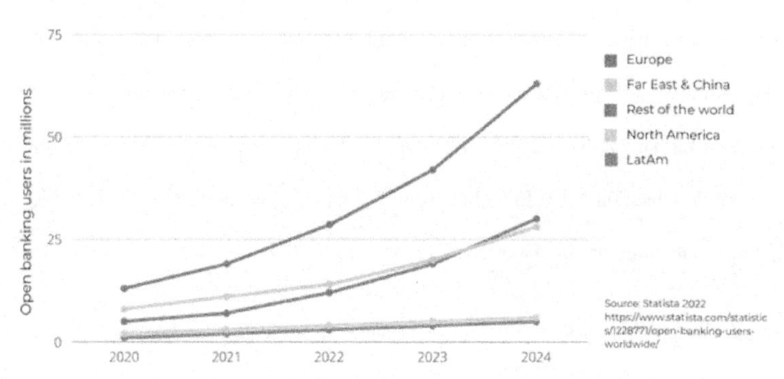

By granting third parties access to consumers' financial data, organisations can better understand how consumers behave, what they want, and most importantly, what they need. In turn, financial institutions can therefore improve their customer experience, which results in higher retention and engagement.

According to PWC, the "retail customer propositions that are enabled or enhanced by Open Banking will include:

- Account aggregation to provide single view of accounts across different banks
- Financial management tools using data analytics to identify spending patterns to budget and save more effectively
- Tailored product offerings based on transaction history, such as customised holiday loans based on flight and hotel bookings and anticipated spend
- Increased access to credit for 'thin-file' customers due to improved access to financial data"

PwC goes on to state that Open Banking has created a £7.2 billion revenue opportunity. Financial institutions are beginning to act as they look to embrace this opportunity. 47% of banks developed Open Banking APIs in 2021, with another 25% following suit in 2022. In addition, this momentum has been furthered by political action, such as President Biden's Executive Order on Promoting Competition in the American Economy.

Expect Open Banking to dominate the financial services sector in 2023 and beyond.

2. Cloud-native systems will replace legacy alternatives

Leading financial organisations continue to embrace cloud-native systems. For example, in 2020, HSBC signed a long-term deal with Amazon Web Services to move their existing legacy functions over to new cloud-based alternatives. And then there's Deutsche Bank, which partnered with Google to deliver a cloud-native "fully-managed environment for applications".

But why is the cloud so important? According to IBM, cloud-based systems support increased agility, decrease IT costs and operational expenses, and play a key role in ensuring that employees can be effective when working remotely.

This last point is especially important. Hybrid working is the future—in fact, 90% of employees surveyed by Loom are happier with the increased freedom that working from home gives them. By leveraging cloud-native systems, employees can access crucial financial data at any time and any place. With cloud-native capabilities, financial institutions can maintain high performance at all times and dramatically improve both customers' and employees' satisfaction.

Cloud-native architecture and systems also enable faster new feature development and automatic upgrades (instead of disruptive updates that require downtime).

3. Artificial intelligence and machine learning will increase in importance

Artificial intelligence (AI) and machine learning (ML) make organisations more efficient and more effective. These technologies gather, sort, and analyse enormous datasets in seconds—and are almost error-free. Financial institutions can spend their time acting on these data-driven insights, instead of wasting unnecessary time and effort manually digging through the data itself.

IDC predicts that by 2026, 85% of organisations will use AI and ML in some capacity to augment their foresight, resulting in a 25% increase in productivity. Low-code/no-code AI is a great example, allowing people without coding knowledge to build applications themselves. While Gartner reported that "low-code tools will make up 65 percent of all app development by 2024", Forrester also outlined that low-code/no-code industry spending was on track to reach approximately $21 billion by this 2022.

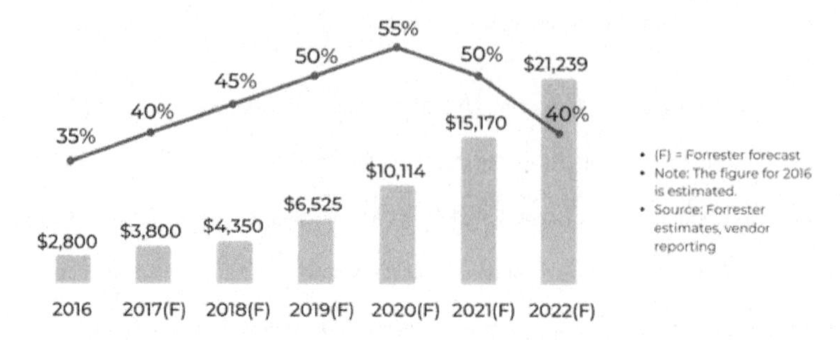

Whether these technologies are used to personalise service offerings, better understand consumers' behaviour, or reduce errors, one thing is for certain: AI and ML will only grow in importance moving forward.

4. Cybersecurity will become a top priority

Cybersecurity has always been crucial for financial institutions. However, with the number of data breaches up until the 30th of September 2021 exceeding the total number of events throughout 2020 by 17%, it's clearly more of a concern than ever before. These cyber attacks have a wide-ranging impact on organisations. In fact, 42% of businesses say that digital fraud prevents innovation and halts their expansion into new channels.

Cybersecurity breaches are particularly damaging for financial institutions. Their customers' financial and personally identifiable information (PII) are incredibly valuable for hackers—and security breaches may well result in the bank losing a huge quantity of customers as well as revenue.

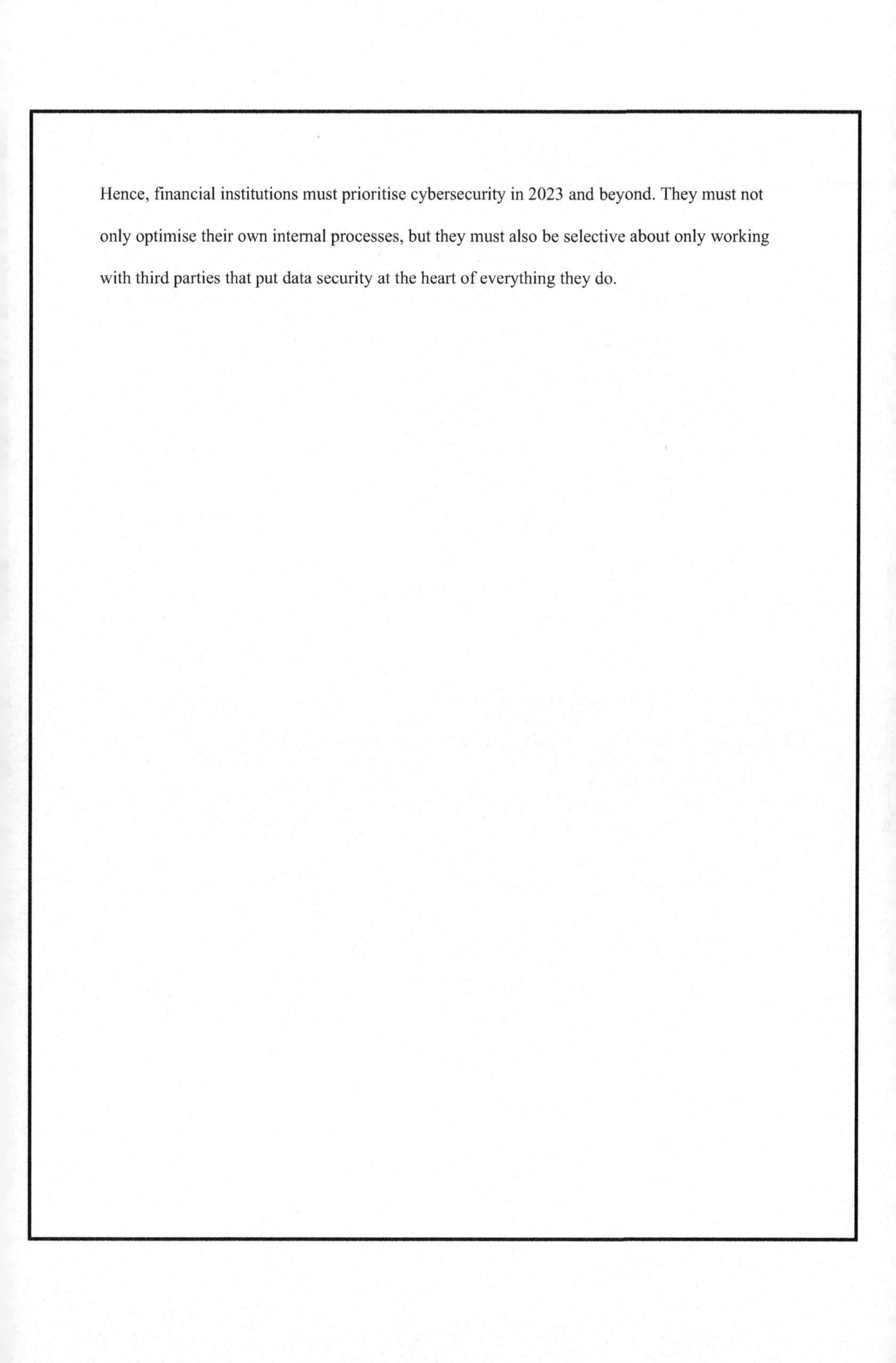

Hence, financial institutions must prioritise cybersecurity in 2023 and beyond. They must not only optimise their own internal processes, but they must also be selective about only working with third parties that put data security at the heart of everything they do.

10: SPREAD BETTING IN THE UK

Spread betting is a financial derivative that enables you to bet on the future direction of financial markets instead of taking ownership of the assets themselves. It gets its name from the spread, or the difference between the buy and sell prices you'll pay when you trade.

There are several benefits that come with spread betting. You can utilise leverage, which means you don't have to pay for the full value of your position – you just need a deposit called your margin. You can go long or short on 1,000s of markets across FX, stocks, indices, commodities and more. And in the UK, spread betting is completely tax free.

How Does Spread Betting Work?

Spread betting works by tracking the value of an asset, so that you can take a position on the underlying market price – without taking ownership of the asset. There are a few key concepts about spread betting you need to know, including:

1. Short and long trading
2. Leverage
3. Margin

What do 'long' and 'short' mean in spread betting?

Going long is the term used to describe placing a bet that the market price will increase over a certain timeframe. Going short or 'shorting' a market is the reverse – placing a bet that the market will decline.

So spread betting enables you to speculate on both rising and falling markets. You would buy the market to go long, or sell the market to go short.

Let's say you thought the price of gold was going to decline. You could open a spread bet to 'sell' the underlying market. The loss or gain to your position would depend on the extent to which your prediction was correct. If the market did decline, your spread bet would profit. But if the price of gold increased instead, your position would make a loss.

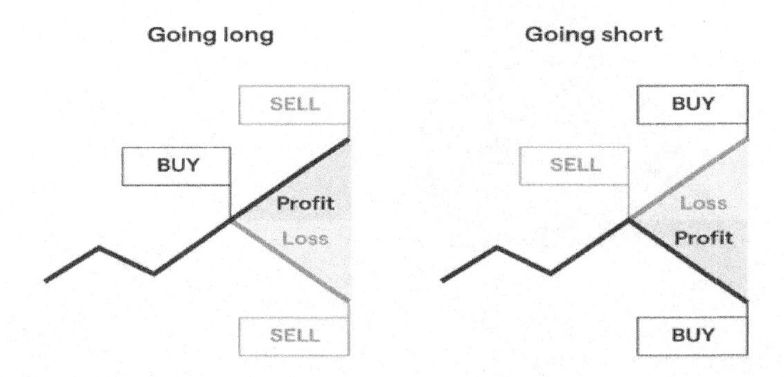

What is leverage in spread betting?

Leverage enables you to gain full market exposure for a fraction of the underlying market cost.

Say you wanted to open a position on Facebook shares. As an investor that would mean paying the full cost of the shares upfront. But by spread betting on Facebook shares instead, you might only have to put down a deposit worth 20% of the cost.

It's important to note that leverage magnifies both profits and losses as these are calculated based on the full value of the position, not just the initial deposit. To manage your exposure, you should create a suitable risk management strategy and to consider how much capital you can afford to put at risk.

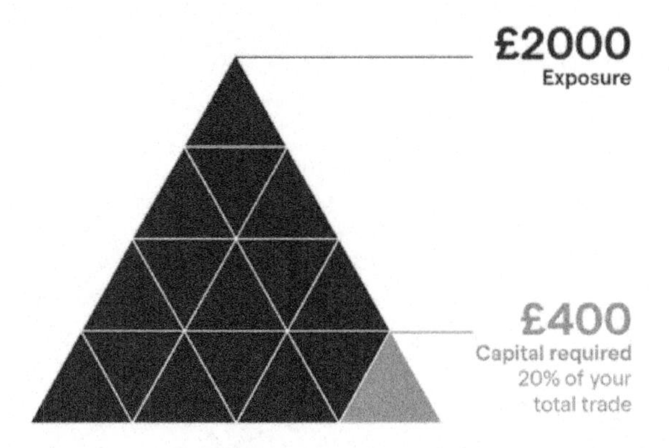

What is margin in spread betting?

When you spread bet, you put down a small initial deposit – known as the margin – to open a position. This is why leveraged trading is sometimes referred to as 'trading on margin'.

There are two types of margin to consider when spread betting:

1. **Deposit margin**. This is the initial funding required to open the position, which is usually presented as a percentage of your total trade.
2. **Maintenance margin**. This refers to the additional funds that might be required if your open position starts to incur losses that are not covered by the initial deposit. You'll get a

notification – known as a margin call – asking you to top up the funds or risk having your position closed

Your margin rate when spread betting depends on the market you trade. For example, when you spread bet on shares your margin might be 20% of the trade size. Whereas, if you spread bet on forex, it might be just 3.33% of the trade size. See our margin rates.

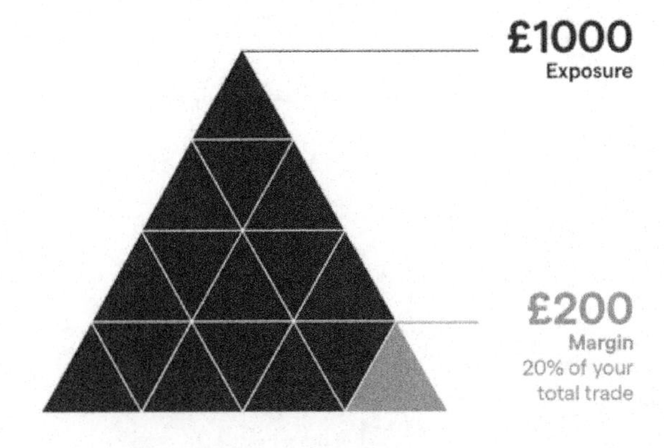

Main features of spread betting

Spread betting has three main features: the spread, bet size and bet duration. The spread is the charge you'll pay for a position, the bet size is the amount of money you want to put up per point of market movement, and the bet duration is how long your position will remain open before it expires.

1. The spread
2. The bet size

3. The bet duration

What is the spread?

The spread is the difference between the buy and sell prices, which are wrapped around the underlying market price. They're also known as the offer and bid. The costs of any given trade are factored into these two prices, so you'll always buy slightly higher than the market price and sell slightly below it.

For example, if the FTSE 100 is trading at 5885.5 and has a one-point spread, it would have an offer price of 5886 and a bid price of 5885.

What is the bet size?

The bet size is the amount you want to bet per unit of movement of the underlying market. You can choose your bet size, as long as it meets the minimum we accept for that market. Your profit or loss is calculated as the difference between the opening price and the closing price of the market, multiplied by the value of your bet.

We measure the price movements of the underlying market in points. Depending on the liquidity and volatility of your chosen market, a point of movement can represent a pound, a penny, or even a one hundredth of a penny. You can find out what a point means for your chosen market on the deal ticket.

If you open a £2 per point bet on the FTSE 100 and it moves 60 points in your favour, your profit would be £120 (£2 x 60). If it moved 60 points against you, your loss would be £120.

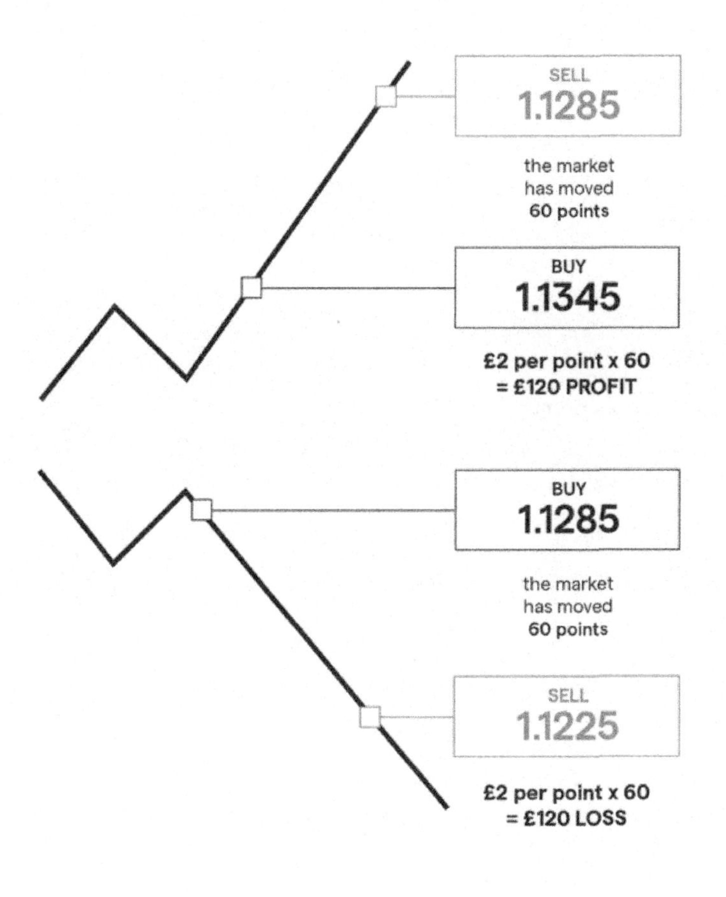

What is the bet duration?

The bet duration is the length of time before your position expires. All spread bets have a fixed timescale that can range from a day to several months away. You're free to close them at any point before the designated expiry time, assuming the spread bet is open for trading.

Our spread bet durations include:

- **Daily funded bets**. These bets run for as long as you choose to keep them open, with a default expiry in the distant future. They offer our tightest spreads but are subject to overnight funding – so are generally used for short-term positions
- **Quarterly bets**. These are futures bets that expire at the end of a quarterly period – although they can be rolled into the next quarter if you let us know in advance. They have wider spreads, but lower funding costs that are built into the price, making them suitable for longer-term speculation

Advantages of Spread Betting

Spread betting is attractive largely because it has a number of key advantages over other forms of trading. The traditional basis for comparison is trading in shares, and spread betting almost objectively presents a more attractive option for investment with lower trading costs, higher returns and a more favourable tax treatment in the UK. But even when compared to derivatives and other highly leveraged investment opportunities, the advantage of spread betting give it serious clout as a trading style, and justify its rise as one of the most popular ways to play the markets – amongst both individual and institutional investors alike.

The advantages of spread betting are multiple and diverse, and as market innovations go it's probably one of the more clever investment product developments of the last century. We've taken each of the key benefits in turn to explain exactly why and how spread betting can work for you: Leverage, Tax Treatment, Simplicity, Flexibility, Range of Markets, Costs, Execution, Currency Exposure.

Advantage of Leverage

Arguable the core advantage of spread betting, transactions are highly leveraged by their very nature. A one point movement would yield insignificant proportional returns in a share or commodity market for a direct trade. With spread betting, however, one point delivers a 100% return on the initial stake, with each additional point represent another full multiple of the original stake amount. And with the possibility of broker credit, leverage can be applied to deliver substantial returns in a short period of time, lending spread betting to both individual and organisational traders as an alternative to more traditional instruments.

Tax Treatment

In addition to the built-in leverage factor, spread betting is dealt a favourable hand by the UK tax authorities. Because there is no physical transaction, spread betting is completely free of capital gains tax (which would otherwise be applicable to the trading of shares or commodities directly), and free of the stamp duty that is levied on share transactions. This can amount to a significant saving on individual transactions, and represents an even more considerable saving over time when aggregated over a number of different trades. These tax savings add up to more money in your pocket, and making grinding a profit from your trading a more achieveable goal.

Simple Transaction Structure

Unlike derivatives and other trading instruments which can give rise to particularly complex transactions and calculations, spread betting is essentially quite simple. If a market moves up by 10 points, you get 10 times your per point stake in return. If a market moves down 10 points, you lose 10 times your stake. For traders making split second investment decisions, the ease with which a spread betting transaction can be sized up makes it more amenable to quick calculations and therefore more immediate trading decisions.

Flexibility Of Financial Spread Betting

Spread betting is also an inherently flexible way of getting involved in the markets, allowing you to profit from both the upside and downside of different indices over varying periods of time. One of the main ways in which this flexibility can be put to best use is through hedging, whereby risks of other positions can be offset by taking conversely related positions in order to ideally deliver a profit in all eventualities. Because different markets can be simultaneously bought and sold, this makes it possible to more effectively manage risks while profiting from a diverse range of markets.

Wide Range Of Markets

Alongside the flexibility of the instrument itself, financial spread betting companies also offer a broad range of markets to spread bet on, including some which are inaccessible through other investment vehicles. For example, traders may be able to invest in markets for differential pairings, which work on the basis of the difference between two stock/market prices, or may be able to back interest rates or even some economic indicators. This additional scope allows traders to diversify their portfolio to a greater extent, and capitalise on a broader base of trading opportunities as a result.

Lower Barriers To Entry

Spread betting allows traders to get involved in trading multiple markets, with buy-ins starting at just £1.00 per point. This ultimately makes spread betting more accessible, and allows traders to invest according to their own budget, rather than according to the market rate and standard contract sizes. This adds to the flexibility, and allows traders to back positions based on profit potential, rather than market prices.

Instant Execution

Because spread betting doesn't take place on an exchange, it lends itself to faster transaction execution times. This results in virtually instant execution, which has a knock on effect on profitability. With fast moving, volatile markets, every second counts, and a trade that is set to close out in profit can easily decay in the time between making the order and its actual execution on the market. With fast dealing timescales comes more responsive trading, and helps give traders peace of mind that the trading decisions they make can be best reflected in their trading bottom line.

Mitigate Currency Exposure

An advantage that perhaps doesn't immediately spring to mind, spread betting also protects against the effects of your exposure to currency fluctuations when dealing in assets denominated in a foreign currency. Fluctuations in the currency market can eat away at your profit portions and are often subject to less than competitive exchange rates in the hands of brokers. Spread betting, on the other hand, is always denominated in your base currency and therefore provides an immunity to the risks of currency rate changes.

While these are just a few of the key benefits of trading through financial spread betting, there are many more different advantages and perks that come with the territory as a spread bettor. As a result, spread betting has adopted an almost viral nature in its spread throughout financial spheres, making it a popular choice amongst both individual traders and the large institutional investors alike.

11: FUTURES AND OPTIONS

If there's one thing that's certain about financial and commodity markets, it's price changes. Prices keep changing all the time. They can go up and down in response to various factors, including the state of the economy, the weather, agricultural production, election results, coups, wars and government policies. The list is practically endless.

Naturally, those who are dealing in these markets will be concerned about price fluctuations, since changes in prices can mean losses – or profits. To protect themselves, they resort to derivatives like futures and options. A derivative is a contract which derives its value from underlying assets; the underlying assets could include stocks, commodities, currency, and so on.

What are futures?

One type of derivative is the futures contract. In this type of contract, a buyer (or seller) agrees to buy (or sell) a certain quantity of a particular asset, at a specific price at a future date.

Let's illustrate this with an example. Let's say you have bought a futures contract to buy 100 shares of Company ABC at Rs 50 each at a specific date. At the expiry of the contract, you will get those shares are Rs 50, irrespective of the current prevailing price. Even if the price goes up to Rs 60, you will get the shares at Rs 50 each, which means you make a neat profit of Rs 1,000. If the share price falls to Rs 40, however, you will still have to buy them at Rs 50 each. In which case you will make a loss of Rs 1,000! Stocks are not the only asset in which futures are available. You can get futures contracts for agricultural commodities, petroleum, gold, currency etc.

Futures are invaluable in helping escape the risk of price fluctuations. A country that is importing oil, for instance, will buy oil futures to insulate itself from price increases in the future. Similarly, farmers will lock in prices of their products using futures so that they don't have to run the risk of a fall in prices when they are ready to sell their harvest.

What are options?

Another kind of derivative is the options contract. This is a little different from a futures contract in that it gives a buyer (or seller) the *right*, but not the *obligation*, to buy (or sell) a particular asset at a certain price at a specific pre-determined date.

There are two types of options: the call option and the put option. A call option is a contract that gives the buyer the right, but not the obligation, to buy a particular asset at a specified price on a specific date. Let's say you have purchased a call option to buy 100 shares of Company ABC at Rs 50 each on a certain date. But the share price falls to Rs 40 below the end of the expiry period, and you have no interest in going through with the contract because you will be making losses. You then have the right not to buy the shares at Rs 50. Hence instead of losing Rs 1,000 on the deal, your only losses will be the premium paid to enter into the contract, which will be much lower.

Another type of option is the put option. In this type of contract, you can sell assets at an agreed price in the future, but not the obligation. For instance, if you have a put option to sell shares of Company ABC at Rs 50 at a future date, and share prices rise to Rs 60 before the expiry date, you have the option of not selling the share for Rs 50. So you would have avoided a loss of Rs 1,000.

What is future and option trading?

One advantage of futures and options is that you can freely trade these on various exchanges. E.g. you can trade stock futures and options on stock exchanges, commodities on commodity exchanges, and so on. While learning about what is F&O trading, it's essential to understand that you can do so without taking possession of the underlying asset. While you may not be interested in purchasing gold per se, you can still take advantage of price fluctuations in the commodities by investing in gold futures and options. You will need much less capital to profit from these price changes.

How to Trade Futures and Options

Trading in F&O or Futures and Options requires specific knowledge and skills. One needs to have sharp clarity on basic concepts like fundamental analysis, technical analysis, F&O

strategies, and the different put and call options. This trading is a tad bit more complex than equity investments, so you need to understand its nuances before you begin trading. The derivatives market is one unique segment of the equity market, containing F&O or Futures and Options.

Unlike stocks, which can be directly traded on the stock market, derivatives are those instruments that lack a present value. They indicate the underlying asset's price, and you can place your opinion on its future price. Trading in derivative products like Futures and Options is like speculating on the value of pre-existing instruments (e.g., Gold, stocks, bonds).

Futures and Options Differences

Although both are derivative products, there is a fundamental difference between Futures and Options. Futures are an obligation for both the buyer and seller, where they have to trade at a pre-established value of the underlying asset. In contrast, Options are not obligations, but a right of the buyer, where they can trade at a pre-established price of the underlying security.

To simplify this further, when the buyer enters into a futures contract with the seller, they forge an agreement to buy and sell the asset respectively at a specified time in the future at a particular price. Thus, the buyer has an obligation to buy the assets as per the agreement. It can be thought of as a commitment that must be fulfilled and squared off at the specified date.

With an options contract, the buyer agrees to buy the asset only at a fixed price, but is not obligated to do so. It is an option buyer's right to exercise or not exercise the contract.

For instance, if any transportation company wants to avoid bearing an unexpected fuel price rise, they can buy futures contracts. A seller can sell these contracts to protect themselves against an unexpected fuel price fall. Here these parties are hedgers or real companies, and fuel is their business base. They agree on the price and quantity of fuel and delivery date.

Before we dive deep into how to trade in f & o and understand how the F&O process works, let's understand some of the commonly used terms in in the derivatives market:

Call Option: The call option gives the buyer the right to buy an underlying asset at a specific price on or before the expiration date

Put Option: The put option gives the buyer the right to sell an underlying asset at a specific price on or before the expiration date

Spot Option: The spot price is the current or present price of the asset in the market

Strike: The strike price is the price at which the buyer and the seller decide to buy or sell the asset after a particular time period

Option Expiry: The day of the expiration of the Options contract which is the last Thursday of each month

Option Premium: A non-refundable premium paid by the Options buyer to the Options seller.

How to Trade in F&O

To begin trading in F&O, you can follow the following process.

Step 1: The primary step to begin trading and understanding how to trade in futures and options is to create a trading account with a broker where you can buy and sell Futures & Options contracts. These contracts are bought via BSE or NSE registered broking firms.

Step 2: Once your account is created, you have to log on to the portal. You can also choose the mobile application option and browse through the various F&O options available.

Step 3: After picking a platform do some research on which futures and options are available and what suits you better.

Step 4: After finalising your choice, put in the order details, and now you can buy the futures and options at the strike price. It is the price at which a call (option contract owner buys the underlying security at this price) or put option (option contract owner sells the underlying security at this price) is exercised. You buy a Call Option or sell a Put Option if you predict the prices to rise, and vice versa if you predict the price to go down.

Step 5: A vital factor that helped negotiate the Futures contract's price is the spot price. Any asset, like currency or commodity, has a current market price. This is the spot price, which helps in the immediate buy or sell of the commodity, and is the base indicator for the Future contract's pricing.

Now that you have bought an Options contract, there are three outcomes to it to help you take the next step.

> **Offset the position:** Offsetting the position is when the options contract is sold to close the position before the expiry. The result of this selling may result in profit or loss for the seller depending on the price at which the underlying asset is sold.

Exercise the position: The call options contract can be exercised when the underlying asset's price is above the strike price. In a put option, the same can be done when the underlying asset's price is below the strike price.

The Contract expires Worthless: The options contract expires worthless in a call option when the underlying asset's price expires below the strike price. In a put option, this happens when the underlying asset's price expires above the strike price.

What is Expiry in Futures Contract?

There is a fixed expiry date for F&O contracts. You aren't bound for contract fulfilment for the Options contract, and it will expire after the fixed date. However, for the Futures contracts, you are bound for contract fulfilment on the expiration date. The last working Thursday of a month is the expiration date for both Futures and Options. So, the final step is to fulfil the terms of the contracts.

Things to Keep in Mind

Now that you are aware of the F&O trading process, here are a few things to be mindful of:

Options contracts have a risk limitation to your premium amount, but on the flip side, money-making is also limited. Future margins have a rising tendency when the market is volatile. Margins in Future is the money you need to deposit with the broker on buying a Futures contract. If the margins rise up sharply, you have to put in fresh margins, failing which your broker has to cut down your Futures position. Profit target and stop losses are also important in Futures. Stop losses are advance orders of asset-sell at a particular point, which helps you to limit your loss. The importance of profit targets is huge because your trade exit point determines the profit you make. While trading in F&O, your mindset should be of a trader. Protection of primary capital can be your focus, for which you need to define your profit trade-off and loss for every trade. You must check the costs you are bearing in the F&O trade. For trading in F&O, you will incur brokerage costs, statutory charges, stamp duty, and likewise charges.

The Bottom Line

To begin, F&O trading may come across as a challenge for most people entering the stock market. But, understanding how to trade in Futures and Contracts is not rocket science. The process becomes easier to deal with when you understand the relevant terms and strategies.

CONCLUSION TAKE AWAY

In conclusion, "Financial Markets Simplified: A Journey of Insights" has been an eye-opening exploration of the dynamic and ever-evolving world of finance. Throughout this book, we have delved into the intricacies of global economies, dissected market trends, and unraveled the mysteries behind investment strategies.

Our journey has been one of continuous learning, where we have gained a deeper understanding of the factors that influence financial markets and the principles that govern them. From bull runs to bear markets, we have witnessed the ebb and flow of economic cycles, recognizing that uncertainty is an inevitable companion on this path.

Yet, armed with knowledge and a disciplined approach, we have discovered that opportunities lie amidst the fluctuations. The art of risk management and strategic decision-making has proven to be the compass guiding us through the stormy seas of volatility.

Moreover, we have realized that the essence of financial markets extends far beyond numbers and charts. It is a complex interplay of human behavior, emotions, and perceptions that can sway the course of economic landscapes. Understanding the psychology of markets has been as crucial as analyzing economic indicators.

As we conclude this journey, we must remember that the financial markets are not merely a destination but a continuous voyage of growth and adaptation. The principles we have explored will remain timeless, but the landscape will evolve, presenting new challenges and opportunities.

The key takeaway from this book is the importance of continuous education and a willingness to adapt to change. Whether you are an investor, trader, or financial enthusiast, staying informed and open to innovation is essential for navigating the ever-changing currents of finance.

I extend my heartfelt gratitude to each reader who embarked on this journey with me. May the insights gained from "Navigating the Financial Markets" serve as a guiding light on your personal financial voyage. Remember, with knowledge, determination, and a clear vision, you can navigate the financial markets and set sail towards a prosperous future.

-The End-

Printed in Great Britain
by Amazon